MOUNDVILLE

Alabama
THE FORGE OF HISTORY

A Series of Illustrated Guides

MOUNDVILLE

John H. Blitz

The University of Alabama Press • Tuscaloosa

The University of Alabama Press
Tuscaloosa, Alabama 35487-0380
uapress.ua.edu

Inquiries about reproducing material from this work should be
addressed to the University of Alabama Press.

Typeface: AGaramond

Cover image: *Top*, Mound B; courtesy of the University of Alabama
Museums, photography by Tim Mistovich; *bottom*, artist re-creation
of Moundville; artwork by Steven Patricia, courtesy of the Art
Institute of Chicago

Frontispiece: Moundville site; courtesy of the University of Alabama
Museums

E-ISBN: 978-0-8173-8067-0

Cataloging-in-Publication data is available from the Library of
Congress.
ISBN: 978-0-8173-5478-7

Contents

Illustrations

Table

Acknowledgments

I would like to take this opportunity to thank the people and institutions that assisted me in the preparation of this book.

The following people were most helpful: Mary Bade, William Baston, Bill Bomar, Robert Clouse, David Dye, Eugene Futato, Betsy Gilbert, Jim Knight, Karl Lorenz, Tim Mistovich, Craig Remington, Ted Roberts, Vin Steponaitis, Joe Vogel, Jan Whyllson, and Greg Wilson.

I am grateful for the assistance of the following organizations and institutions: Art Institute of Chicago, Harvard University Archives, Smithsonian Institution National Museum of the American Indian, Riverhill Enterprises, and University of Tennessee Press; and at The University of Alabama, the Alabama Museum of Natural History, Cartographic Research Library, Department of Anthropology, Moundville Archaeological Park, Office of Archaeological Research, The University of Alabama Press, and the W. S. Hoole Special Collections Library.

A special thank you is reserved for Lisa LeCount.

1

Introducing Moundville

Late in the nineteenth century, a farmer was plowing a field near the little town of Carthage, Alabama. Mysterious mounds of earth loomed over the field, monuments of a settlement abandoned so long ago that no one knew who had lived here. The man had often found pottery and stone tools left by the ancient inhabitants, so when the plow struck something hard, he stopped to take a look. The object he lifted from the soil was like nothing he had ever seen before. It was a polished stone disk, perfectly round, about twelve inches in diameter. Small notches were placed all around the edge of the disk. On one side were incised circular lines. On the other side was a strange engraving showing an open human hand with what looked like an eye peering from it. Encircling the hand-and-eye image were two entwined rattlesnakes with horns and long tongues.

The farmer took the disk home. One day a man who said he was a professor at the nearby university came by and wanted to see the relic. The farmer had heard claims that giants, a vanished "Mound-Builder Race," or the Aztecs of Mexico had erected the mounds, and he asked the professor if this was so. The professor, Eugene A. Smith, founder of the

Rattlesnake disk. (Courtesy of The University of Alabama Museums.)

Alabama Museum of Natural History, told the farmer that the U.S. Congress had provided funds to investigate as many mounds as possible to settle the question once and for all. Smith returned to Tuscaloosa with the rattlesnake disk.

The rattlesnake disk was found at the archaeological site of Moundville, near the modern town of that name. Today, visitors to Moundville Archaeological Park often express wonder that such a place exists. Here, along the banks of the Black Warrior River in west Alabama, they can walk among the

Moundville site. (Courtesy of The University of Alabama Museums.)

protected remains of a town founded by American Indians eight hundred years ago. For several centuries prior to the arrival of the Europeans, it was one of the largest settlements north of Mexico. Key features of the 320-acre site are 29 earthen mounds, a central open area or plaza, and a log fortification or palisade that is no longer visible. The natural terrace location for the settlement was artificially leveled and filled to create the plaza. The mounds are composed of basket-loaded soil dug from pits that are now small lakes. Most of the mounds are platforms shaped like flat-topped pyramids, built up over time in a series of construction stages. The mound summits supported buildings with various residential, ceremonial, and mortuary uses. Because construction of the ordered arrangement of mounds, plaza, and palisade began at approximately the same time, it is likely that Moundville was a planned community.

Who Were the People of Moundville?

Since Smith's day, it has been proven that Moundville and other prehistoric sites in Alabama and the United States were built by American Indians. The people who built Moundville had no direct ties to the Aztec, Maya, or other civilizations to the south. For thousands of years, as far back as the last Ice Age, they had lived in North America. True, the corn and some other crops they planted had been domesticated first in Mexico and through the centuries passed north into the Southeast, but this is the only confirmed link to Central America of any consequence. There is no evidence of contact with the Old World civilizations of Europe, Africa, or Asia prior to the arrival of the Spanish in the sixteenth century.[1]

The most common question visitors to Moundville ask is, "Which tribe built the mounds?" to which the archaeologists give the disappointing answer, "We don't know." To the surprise of many, this seemingly simple question has proven the most difficult to answer. For like all prehistoric peoples of North America, whoever built the mounds left no written records. We do not know what they called themselves or the place now known as Moundville. We do not know the names of their heroes or their gods. Undoubtedly, their descendants still exist among the American Indians who live in the Southeast. For this reason, the trail that leads from ancient Moundville to modern people has not gone cold.

Reenactor in Mississippian costume. (Courtesy of The University of Alabama Museums.)

The people of Moundville had legends, songs, and tales that were told through generations, faint echoes of which are still heard in native oral traditions. These traditions are providing clues to help interpret the ancient symbols and images on the rattlesnake disk and other artifacts. One day soon it may be possible, through the science of DNA, to identify living descendants of the Moundville people.

The Story of Moundville

This is the story of Moundville and the people who once lived there. They were much like people everywhere, but their cultural world no longer exists. Each generation shaped Moundville to meet their needs. At various times Moundville was a collection of small houses and cornfields, a fortified capital town, a center for sacred ceremonies, and a vast, empty graveyard. No peoples vanish without a trace, however, and the traces are thick on the ground at Moundville. The Moundville story can only be told through archaeology, the scientific study of extinct societies through the physical remains they left behind—the mounds, the discarded stone tools, the broken pottery, and even the bones of the people themselves. These material things are the puzzle pieces of Moundville's hidden past, but the story is not just about artifacts, for the remains are merely the means by which we tell the tale. Ultimately, the story is not about a place or things but the people who once built a mound, envisioned the beauty of a rattlesnake disk, and ate their meals from a drab cooking pot.

Mounds, disks, and pots do not speak for themselves. The challenge of archaeology is not just to find the evidence but how to interpret it. So this story is also about the people who preserved Moundville and sought ways to tell Moundville's story through archaeology. This is the story of Moundville: what we know about the lives of the long-dead people who once called it home and the scientific saga of the modern people who brought the story to life.

2

Revealing Moundville's Mysteries

Like the lives of people, the history of a dead town is a series of changes: foundation, growth, maturity, decline, and, sometimes, abandonment and forgetting. People erect monuments to extend memory beyond a human lifetime. Moundville's monumental mounds stand as reminders that this was once a place of importance. Ancient monuments commemorate the dead and invite rediscovery by the living. Monuments make the past live in the present. It is appropriate, therefore, that our story begins with a resurrection of sorts.

Monolithic stone ax found at Moundville in the nineteenth century. (Courtesy of National Museum of the American Indian.)

Giants and Mound Builders

In 1866, Sheriff Hezekiah K. Powell announced that he had unearthed a giant from the mounds at Carthage.[1] The skeleton, he claimed, measured nine feet from head to toe. Upon hearing of the discovery, Thomas Maxwell, a local planter, hastened to buy the skeleton, only to learn that Powell had sold the discovery to a Mr. Force, who supposedly had taken it to the Smithsonian Institution in Washington, D.C. Maxwell had long been interested in the Carthage Mounds, having first dug there in 1840. In a paper read before the Alabama Historical Society, he reported that there were fifteen mounds in the group, encircled by an earthwork embankment. Maxwell spent several days digging in one of the mounds, finding bits of pottery and arrowheads, and persisted "until the neighbors thought I was demented."[2]

Such was the state of archaeology in nineteenth-century America, when the question, "Who built the mounds?" was a matter of intense debate.[3] The list of suspects was long: denizens of Atlantis, lost tribes of Israelites, Antediluvians, the Spanish conquistadores, Vikings, Phoenicians, Irish monks, Egyptians, Aztecs, Toltecs, and others. Maxwell supported the most popular theory of the day, that an industrious race of "Mound Builders" had erected the mounds that dotted the great river valleys, only to be wiped out by the arrival of the American Indians. That Powell had found a giant was not exceptional. People were digging up giants all across rural America, in keeping with the scriptural wisdom that "There were giants in the earth in those days" (Gen. 6:4).

Moundville in the early twentieth century. (Courtesy of
The University of Alabama Museums.)

Perhaps stimulated by Powell's discovery,
Nathaniel T. Lupton, a scientist and later the fifth
president of The University of Alabama, undertook
his own investigation of the mounds near Carthage.[4]
Lupton gave more attention to observation and
measurement than did Maxwell. He produced a rea-
sonably accurate map of the site, recorded the location and depth of his excavations in one of the
mounds (later labeled Mound O), and sent his finds
to the Smithsonian Institution.

In the 1880s, the U.S. government entered the
mound builder debate. The Division of Mound
Exploration sent agents to excavate mound sites and
synthesize the results of the great Mound Survey.
One of these agents conducted a brief, poorly documented investigation at the Moundville site in
1882.[5] This effort deemed inadequate, a second
Mound Survey agent, Edward Palmer, sought per-

Nathaniel T. Lupton. (Courtesy of the W. S. Hoole Special Collections Library, The University of Alabama.)

mission to dig at the site the following year. The landowner demanded $100 for the privilege. The cost was too high for the government, and Palmer left empty-handed. After investigating dozens of mound sites, the Division of Mound Exploration published their findings in 1894, concluding that the mound builders were American Indians. The fledgling science of archaeology won an important scholarly victory, but Moundville, one of the largest of the mound sites, is not mentioned anywhere in the Mound Survey report.

The *Gopher of Philadelphia*

One day in 1905, a steamboat named *Gopher of Philadelphia* tied up near Moundville. The *Gopher* carried a photographic darkroom, picks and shovels, a trained crew of diggers, and comfortable lodgings for her owner, Clarence B. Moore.[6] Moore was a gentleman archaeologist, a wealthy Philadelphian with an obsession for digging up ancient Indian artifacts. Heir to a paper company fortune and a lifelong bachelor, Moore was free to mount annual collecting expeditions on a grand scale. During the cooler months of each year beginning in 1891, Moore and his companion, Dr. Milo Miller, plied the rivers of the Southeast. The expeditions always proceeded in the same manner. Hired agents located sites and secured the landowner's permission to dig. The advance work finished, Moore boarded the *Gopher*. Then, one by one, the boat stopped at prehistoric mound and village sites along a southern river. The crew dug a series of "trial holes" until they located graves and the artifacts they contained. When he returned to Philadelphia, Moore wrote a lavishly illustrated catalog of his finds for the *Journal of the Academy of Natural Sciences of Philadelphia*. The academy sponsored Moore, but he financed the operation. Now Moore had arrived at Moundville. He would not be disappointed.

Moore spent thirty-five days at the site and then returned the next year for about a month.[7] Dr. Miller mapped the site, recorded the heights of the mounds, and assigned letters to each mound. Moore's crew fanned out over the site, digging several hundred trial holes about four feet wide and four

Clarence B. Moore. (Courtesy of Harvard University Archives, call# HUP Moore, Clarence B. [1].)

feet deep. When burials, whole pots, or interesting artifacts were uncovered, the holes were expanded in size. Soon trial holes were in almost all of the mounds and in some open fields near mounds. Moore's trial holes detected three kinds of deposits: mounds without burials, mounds with burials, and residential areas near mounds with deep accumulations of midden (piles of discarded food remains and artifacts) with graves. Moore labeled mounds without burials "domiciliary," meaning they had been put to residential or some use other than as a burial place. Once Moore pronounced a mound "domiciliary," digging ceased and the crew moved on looking for graves. Moore noted that mounds

The *Gopher of Philadelphia.*

with burials had first served some other purpose; later, "superficial" graves dug from the summit surface pierced the mound. After these funerals, the builders added a new mound construction layer to cover the old mound summit. Mounds C, D, and O, and midden areas north and south of Mounds D and R produced the most burials and, consequently, the greatest quantity of artifacts accompanying the skeletons.

Moundville rewarded Moore's efforts with some of the most beautiful and impressive prehistoric artifacts ever found in the Southeast. The midden ridge north of R (Mound U) produced an astounding bowl in the shape of a birdlike creature, carved from a solid piece of diorite stone. Large stone smoking pipes were discovered in several locations; one from Mound U was in the shape of a catlike monster, and

Serpent-bird effigy stone bowl. (Courtesy of
National Museum of the American Indian.)

another from Mound O depicted a squatting
human. Moore found round and rectangular incised
stone palettes (the same kind of artifact as the rattlesnake disk) smeared with paint pigments. The
most astonishing burials were uncovered in Mounds
C and D. Here, elaborate ornaments adorned the
skeletons: pendants, badges, hairpins, and gorgets
(circular ornaments worn on the chest) made from
copper foil and embossed with strange designs. Other burials had copper earplugs, copper-bladed axes,
incised shell gorgets, beads of pearls, shell, and copper, and other objects. The two expeditions recovered more than three hundred pottery vessels,
almost all found as burial accompaniments. Many
of these pots are a wide-mouthed bottle distinctive
to Moundville, glossy black and engraved with intri-
cate images of winged serpents, falcons, crested
birds, spirals, scrolls, bones, and skulls. Moore's
finds caused a sensation when his publicist at the
academy, Harriet Wardle, wrote a romantic account

Above: Limestone "cat" pipe. (Courtesy of National Museum of the American Indian.)

Left: Flint-clay human effigy pipe. (Courtesy of National Museum of the American Indian.)

of the discoveries, "The Treasures of Prehistoric Moundville," for the popular magazine *Harper's Monthly.*[8]

By the time of his last expedition in 1918, Moore had dug into hundreds of sites, produced his long series of volumes, and traveled thousands of miles along every navigable waterway in the Deep South.

Above: Circular stone palette. Diameter 26 cm.
Below: Rectangular stone palette. Length 35.5 cm.

Clockwise from top left:
Hair ornament of sheet copper with bone pin in place.
Length 26 cm.

Oblong copper pendant. (Courtesy of National Museum
of the American Indian.)

Shell gorget with engraved human head. (Courtesy of
National Museum of the American Indian.)

Above: Fragment of shell cup. (Courtesy of National Museum of the American Indian.)

Below: Pottery bottle with engraved "crested bird" image. (Courtesy of National Museum of the American Indian.)

Figure 2.16. Pottery bottle with engraved "raptor" and "hand-and-eye" image. (Courtesy of National Museum of the American Indian.)

Unlike treasure hunters, he documented his activities, and monetary gain was not his goal. He did not keep his finds; he donated them to museums all over the United States. Moore sought out various specialists to identify materials. Sometimes he offered cautious interpretations. He concluded that Moundville was a prehistoric center of religious cult activity; it was a planned community; the largest mounds, A and B, had ceremonial purposes; and he identified mounds with burial and residential functions.[9] Moore admired the artistry expressed in the ancient objects and sought to bring these achievements to light. He left a record of long-vanished archaeological sites that still informs modern researchers. Unlike other early archaeologists, however, Moore made little effort to classify and compare his finds by art styles, or to order the artifacts in time, or to present them in a way that would depict prehistoric cultures. He was content to describe and illustrate. Moore was, first and last, a collector, and a very methodical one at that. It would fall to others to seek ancient objects at Moundville for a more ambitious goal: to reconstruct a past way of life.

Dr. Jones and the CCC Boys

Moore's remarkable discoveries attracted treasure hunters to Moundville. The Alabama State Antiquities Law, in part a response to digging at Moundville by Moore and others, was passed in 1915.[10] The law limited excavation of archaeological sites to state officials and prohibited exportation of artifacts out of the state. In 1923, Clara Powers of the Moundville Historical Society and other citizens began a campaign to establish Moundville as a state park.[11] An aged C. B. Moore gave encouragement, but no money. The site gained the interest of a young geologist at The University of Alabama, Dr. Walter B. Jones. Upon succeeding Eugene A. Smith as director of the Alabama Museum of Natural History (AMNH), Jones saw an opportunity. Efforts to get the lethargic state government to acquire the site stalled, so Dr. Jones made a plea to the AMNH Board of Regents to purchase Moundville, stating, "We robbed the Indians of everything they had, and the least we can do is to preserve this wonderful monument which they left behind."[12]

Walter B. Jones. (Courtesy of the W. S. Hoole Special Collections Library, The University of Alabama.)

Swayed by Jones's vision, the AMNH began to buy portions of the site. The Alabama Department of Archives and History, suddenly stirred into action by this new development, asserted that it alone had the authority to administer historic places like Moundville. Archives and History personnel attempted to block the sale but failed.[13] No sooner was this obstacle to Jones's plan averted when a new threat appeared. The Great Depression descended upon the country, it hit Alabama hard, and no one had money. Undaunted, Jones made more purchases with his personal funds, at one point mortgaging his home for extra cash. By 1933, the site was Mound State Park, owned and administered by AMNH.

Desperate poverty gripped the region in the 1930s.[14] One of President Roosevelt's public relief programs, the Civilian Conservation Corps (CCC), provided a lifeline to unemployed men. Beginning in 1934, Jones managed to acquire small groups of "CCC boys" to work on improvements to the site. By 1938, Moundville had a CCC camp of two hundred men.[15] The workers planted trees, patched eroded mounds, and cleared ponds of silt. Soon Jones had a staff of archaeologists supervising a large CCC labor force in extensive excavations. Whereas Moore had concentrated most of his work on the mounds, the CCC excavations focused on other areas of the site, especially at the location of a planned museum and along the path of the park's roadway. In 1938, Mound State Park was renamed Mound State Monument. The CCC–constructed Archaeological Museum opened the following year. A beautiful little building in Art Deco style, it featured the novel presentation of human burials left preserved in place for public viewing. A cast of more than one thousand costumed citizens and CCC boys staged an outdoor pageant, *Children of the Sun God,* at the park.[16] With America's entry into World War II, the camp at Moundville disbanded as the CCC boys exchanged their work denims for military fatigues. The Depression excavations had resulted in the excavation of 75 house remains, 2,050 burials, and thousands of artifacts.[17] Dr. Jones fulfilled his dream of a protected Moundville where visitors could learn about the prehistoric peoples of Alabama.

Above: A "CCC boy." (Courtesy of The University of Alabama Museums.)

Below: CCC workers excavate house remains at Moundville, 1930s. (Courtesy of The University of Alabama Museums.)

Children of the Sun God pageant, 1939. (Courtesy of Jan Whyllson.)

"The DeJarnette Phase"

In 1929, as a new round of investigations began at Moundville, David L. DeJarnette became Dr. Jones's right-hand man.[18] A hard-eyed pragmatist and energetic organizer, DeJarnette was to become a pivotal figure in Alabama archaeology.[19] Trained as an electrical engineer at The University of Alabama, DeJarnette was soon leading the AMNH excavations. At

first these digs were artifact hunts modeled after
Moore's expeditions, searches for pots and other
items to place on exhibit. The antiquated methods
of Moore's day were inadequate, so Jones sent
DeJarnette to Illinois for training with a new generation of archaeologists at a University of Chicago
"field school" for archaeological techniques. Return-
ing to Alabama, DeJarnette and Jones launched the
modern era of Alabama archaeology.

DeJarnette instituted archaeological techniques
that are standard procedure in modern excavations.
Three concepts guide archaeological field methods:
provenience (the location of the finds), association
(materials found together), and context (the cultural
significance of the finds as interpreted from the evidence of provenience and association). Archaeologists must dig in a way to record provenience, association, and context. To remove objects without
recording these relationships results in lost information. Maps record provenience by showing artifact
location, measuring horizontally across an archaeological site and vertically down into the ground as
the digging progresses. To document association,
archaeologists keep objects found in the same deposit
layer, grave, ruined house, or other feature together,
separate from other finds. Just as detectives at a crime
scene use similar concepts to reconstruct activities
they did not witness themselves, so too must archaeologists proceed slowly and carefully, recording
provenience and association as they go. Provenience
and association, along with other clues, help archaeologists interpret the context of the finds and make
informed statements about prehistoric life.

David L. DeJarnette. (Courtesy of V. J. Knight.)

Archaeology requires trained teams to do the digging, sifting of soil, bagging, labeling, photograph-
ing, and drawing. Once the artifacts are out of the
ground the laboratory process begins, washing, sort-
ing, and analyzing the materials with various measurements. Someone once quipped that interpreting
an archaeological site is akin to assembling a multi-
dimensional jigsaw puzzle with some of the pieces
missing. All this work is for naught if others never
learn about the finds, so the final task is to write a
report. If all this sounds laborious, tedious, and

Students at Moundville record vertical provenience,
1990s. (Courtesy of V. J. Knight.)

time-consuming, it is. The research is rewarding,
however, for the archaeologist is an explorer in time
and a detective of the past. Slowly, one artifact and
one archaeological site at a time, a picture of what
happened in prehistory comes into focus.

Archaeologists of the 1930s through the 1950s
such as DeJarnette were most concerned with iden-
tifying prehistoric cultures, ordering the cultures
into a time sequence, and charting the distribution
of the ancient cultures on a map. They tallied up
"trait lists" of artifacts for each culture. Because
traits changed through time, archaeologists could
assign cultures to long time spans called periods and
shorter spans called phases.

DeJarnette implemented these procedures in the
Depression projects at Moundville and other sites in

Alabama. Like assembly lines operating in reverse, large crews of men dismantled the archaeological sites by excavation and sent the materials to a laboratory where teams of women processed the artifacts. Soon so much potential information was out of the ground that analysis and report writing fell behind the pace of digging. World War II ended the projects.

After the war, DeJarnette returned to work at AMNH and eventually became curator of Mound State Monument. During this time, a remarkable episode in Moundville's history began. Starting in 1948 and continuing to the end of the century, local citizens used the mounds as stages in a sunrise Easter pageant. Both insider and outsider viewpoints document the history, organization, and meaning of this Christian folk ritual.[20] DeJarnette did not approve of this use of the site, but he could do nothing to prevent it.

A founding member of The University of Alabama's Department of Anthropology, DeJarnette was the leading archaeologist in the state for two decades. With an authoritarian personality and a volatile temper, he ran Mound State Monument "like a fiefdom. He was lord and master and we were the serfs."[21] DeJarnette spent his entire life organizing gangs of rough-hewn men; he could never stop giving orders. He introduced hundreds of students to archaeology and trained the next two generations of archaeologists in Alabama. Students regarded him with a mixture of awe, fear, and loyalty. Truly the "Father of Alabama Archeology," DeJarnette guided the study of Alabama's archaeological sites from a search for pots to the scientific recording of prehistory.

Moundville Easter pageant, 1960s. (Courtesy of Dr. William P. Baston.)

A Man with a Plan

In 1950 the Erskine Ramsay Archaeological Repository opened at Moundville to house materials from the Depression projects. A few years later, DeJarnette began to catalog and organize the massive collection. Although he published several important works, DeJarnette wrote very little about Moundville. Detailed knowledge about Moundville's past remained dormant, stored in dozens of unopened boxes of artifacts and reams of unread excavation notes.

In the mid-1960s Christopher S. Peebles, a graduate student of anthropology, arrived at Moundville.[22] Peebles had an ambitious research plan. Inspired by the "New Archaeology," Peebles was part of a new generation that believed archaeologists could study the extinct societies of prehistory in much the same way as anthropologists studied the social organization and customs of living peoples. The business of archaeology was not finished when ancient cultures were defined by trait lists and sorted into periods and phases. Archaeologists could do more by determining how and why cultures changed over time.

Peebles informed DeJarnette that he wanted to study Moundville's social organization. DeJarnette must have realized the potential in the young man's intelligence, training, and enthusiasm, for he granted Peebles access to the collections. He knew something that Peebles did not know, however, for Peebles was shocked to discover that there were thousands of notes, forms, maps, and photographs from the CCC days. How could he hope to synthesize this avalanche of information without giving up his teaching job and enduring a period of unemployment while he struggled with the records at Moundville? Help arrived in the form of a used copy machine donated to Peebles by a representative of the Xerox Corporation in Tuscaloosa. The previous owner, the Imperial Wizard of the Ku Klux Klan, had returned the machine, angry that the Xerox Company had sponsored the television program *On Black America.* Assisted by his wife, Peebles made several thousand copies of records over a two-week period and then returned to his teaching post with the data.[23]

Between 1971 and 1974, Peebles earned his doctoral degree and published his reconstruction of Moundville's social organization. It is a landmark study in American archaeology.[24] Peebles examined

the records of more than two thousand human burials with this idea in mind: the treatment of people at
the time of their death and funeral reflected their
social status during their lifetime. Peebles used his
skills in statistics and computers to organize the burial information. He grouped burials into similar categories based on their location and the kinds of
items or grave goods placed with the body. He then
assigned a social status to these burial categories.

Peebles divided prehistoric Moundville society
into low-rank groups and high-rank groups. Burials
of most people at Moundville were near their houses
or in middens; these graves contained common
everyday tools such as a cooking pot or stone ax, or
nothing at all. These people appeared to have
achieved their social status through their deeds in
life or just by being an average man, woman, or
child in Moundville society. Another category was
composed of people with a higher social status. Burial for high-rank, elite members of Moundville society was in mounds or in middens near mounds,
accompanied by ornaments of stone, copper, and
shell. Because young children were also in this category, Peebles concluded that they must have inherited their social status at birth because they were too
young to have earned it themselves. Seven adults
uncovered by Moore in Mounds C and D had the
most elaborate funerals at Moundville. These
important people were found with the copper and
shell ornaments that served as badges or insignia of
high rank, as well as the unique copper-bladed axes
that other members of the society did not possess.
Because the axes were too soft to function as tools or

weapons, they were probably symbols of chiefly status. Peebles concluded that these lavish burials were those of the leaders of Moundville. Thus, ancient Moundville society was composed of at least three social categories: low-rank common folk, high-rank elites with inherited status, and the "chiefs" who led the community.

Peebles realized that there was much more to learn from the excavation records. Furthermore, the 1930s excavations had not collected certain kinds of information: food remains, scraps left from making craft goods, carbon for radiocarbon (C^{14}) dating, and many other things that archaeologists now knew how to interpret. There would have to be new digs at Moundville; archaeologists had explored only about 15 percent of the site. Archaeology was entering a new era when the microscope, computer, and test tube would be as important as the shovel, whisk broom, and trowel. With a grant from the National Science Foundation, Peebles returned to Moundville in the late 1970s with a team of graduate students from the University of Michigan to implement the next stage of research. Identification of changing pottery styles and radiocarbon dates now divided the long period of Moundville's occupation into shorter time spans.[25] Archaeologists knew when Moundville had existed as measured in calendar years. Peebles's students recovered food remains to reconstruct the diet and the economy that supported the population.[26] Other students studied the chemical and physical characteristics of human bones, which revealed much about ancient health and nutrition.[27] Other sites up and down the valley

Copper ax from Mound C. Length 19 cm.

produced artifacts of the Moundville culture. Peebles's students examined a sample of these sites and
concluded that Moundville had been an ancient
capital town that governed a hinterland of smaller
sites.[28]

Ongoing Research

These studies, some completed by the students of
Peebles and DeJarnette, and, more recently, the students of those students, are part of the ongoing
research that forms the basis of what we know about
Moundville today. Research at Moundville continues to use artifacts and information from the older
excavations combined with new small-scale digs
conducted to minimize impacts on the preserved
park. As a result of this hard work, the legacy of
Lupton, Moore, Jones, DeJarnette, and Peebles, we
can now tell the Moundville story.

3

Moundville and the Mississippians

Many people think of traditional American Indian culture as timeless and changeless. This idea is false because culture change, either slow or rapid, is a basic human condition. The people of Moundville benefited from a long series of culture changes experienced by the populations throughout what is now the eastern United States or Eastern Woodlands. To understand Moundville, we must first examine life in the Eastern Woodlands in the centuries before Moundville was built. Archaeologists divide Eastern Woodlands prehistory, or the time without written records, into periods of culture change.[1]

- **Paleoindian** (10,000?–8000 B.C.). This time span began with the uncertain date of the first peopling of the Eastern Woodlands near the end of the last Ice Age. Recognized by their distinctive stone spear points, small mobile bands hunted herd animals such as bison and mastodons.

- **Archaic** (8000–1000 B.C.). This long time span began with the onset of modern climate conditions. Using the spear-thrower to hunt deer and other species present today, Archaic peoples found ways to gather and process many kinds of wild foods, especially plant foods, and aquatic foods such as fish and mussels. Inventions included ground stone axes, stone bowls, nets, and dugout canoes. People formed larger settlements in river valleys and along coasts as populations grew. Trade networks linked groups together to acquire stone, shell, and copper as people fashioned ornaments to mark their social status. The first pottery and plant domestication appeared toward the end of this time span.

- **Woodland** (1000 B.C.–A.D. 800). During this time span, populations in the Eastern Woodlands perfected the inventions and practices begun in the Late Archaic period. Native domesticated plants with oily and starchy seeds contributed to the diet, but people continued to rely on wild foods. Ceremonial centers with burial mounds and earthwork enclosures were widely established. Long-distance trade distributed status-marking ornaments and shared symbols of burial-mound ceremonialism. Two important items, the bow and corn (maize), were products developed elsewhere and acquired by local populations late in Woodland times.

Paleoindians. (Courtesy of The University of Alabama Museums.)

Archaic Indians. (Courtesy of The University of Alabama Museums.)

Woodland Indians. (Courtesy of The University of Alabama Museums.)

Mississippian Indians. (Courtesy of The University of Alabama Museums.)

The Mississippians

The people of Moundville were part of an American Indian cultural development known as Mississippian, named for the central Mississippi River valley where this way of life first appeared a little more than a thousand years ago. The Mississippians lived in fortified towns organized by powerful leaders, built earthen mounds, maintained trade networks, engaged in warfare, and shared symbols and rituals. The Mississippians were not a single "tribe" but a collection of societies spread across different regions that shared similar cultural practices.

The Mississippians built larger settlements and lived in more complex societies than did their Woodland ancestors. Bow-and-arrow warfare and reliance on corn as a staple food changed how people lived. The technological differences between Mississippian and Woodland societies were minor compared to changes in the way society was organized. Living in larger settlements created opportunities for new community organizations. The Mississippians developed new ideas, beliefs, and values. Unlike earlier populations, Mississippian societies were divided into families who inherited social privileges and those who did not. Settlements joined together into political territories with permanent offices of leadership or "chiefs."

These changes took place in the central Mississippi River valley during the Emergent Mississippian period (A.D. 800–1000).[2] The new social order proved so successful that by the year 1050, the largest Mississippian settlement, Cahokia, was well established in Illinois near present-day St. Louis.[3] Set among a cluster of large towns with dozens of mounds, Cahokia was the capital of a regional territory with a population that numbered in the thousands. The largest mound, Monk's Mound, is 100 feet tall, covers more than 14 acres, and contains an estimated 22 million cubic feet of soil. The capital's residents acquired hard stone, marine shell, and other raw materials through trade relationships with distant populations that lacked Cahokia's power and influence. Skilled artisans, working part-time in their homes, converted these valuables into everyday tools and special ornaments of social status for the needs of a growing society. Beyond Cahokia, the basic Mississippian settlement organization was a central place with one or more mounds, referred to as a mound center, surrounded by many small family dwellings known as farmsteads, where people produced corn and other surplus goods.

From A.D. 1000 to 1200, populations throughout the Midwest and Southeast began to intensify their corn production, adopt the mound center–farmstead settlement, organize political territories, and practice regional versions of the Mississippian way of life. Over the next several centuries, mound centers rose and fell, linked together by alliance, exchange of goods, and warfare. When the first Spanish explorers encountered Late Mississippian societies in the 1500s, the largest mound centers were abandoned or in decline. Even so, the Spanish saw fortified settlements where powerful chiefs lived on mounds, were carried on litters, wore copper emblems of rank, and maintained political territories.[4] Although the arrival of the Europeans brought new changes, the Mississippian legacy continued into the 1600s in a few groups, such as the Natchez. Europeans wrote descriptions of customs and practices that provide a guide for archaeologists in their efforts to understand the prehistoric Mississippians.[5] These historic descriptions lack detail, however, and do not represent the Mississippian cultures of previous centuries. Archaeology is the only effective means we have to explore prehistory.

The Mississippians created diverse religious, military, and social institutions. However, some of the conditions present in other ancient civilizations are absent in Mississippian societies. Mississippian artistic creations were made for rituals or to mark religious or warrior positions of authority, not as luxuries for a ruling class. While Mississippians had a hierarchy of status and rank in their communities, they did not have bureaucratic states with economic or social classes separated by great differences in wealth. The economy was not highly diversified into specialists supported by a class of food producers. There was no buying or selling in markets. Their technology was relatively simple and accessible to all. They lacked the means to expand food production to support very large populations. There were powerful chiefs, but no classes of aristocrats and peasants. There were warriors, but no standing

armies that conquered regions. The material conditions of life did not differ greatly, whether one
inherited rank or earned it. In short, Mississippians
lived in towns led by religious or warrior chiefs, not
in cities ruled by kings and queens.[6]

Mississippians in West Alabama

Emergent Mississippian societies like those of the
Midwest were not present in west Alabama from
A.D. 800 to 1000. Instead, regional populations continued a Woodland way of life for some time after
the Mississippians established Cahokia and similar
centers farther north. These Late or Terminal Woodland populations in west Alabama began to adopt
Mississippian   cultural   practices   during   A.D.
1000–1150.[7] Terminal Woodland groups increased
their production of corn and increased the amount
of deer in their diet, changes that maintained rapid
population growth. As these populations grew in
size, trade increased, as did competition between
groups. Small stone drills called microliths, used to
make marine-shell beads, appear at regional sites at
this time. Terminal Woodland groups in west Alabama began to participate in trade networks that
sent vast quantities of marine shell north to Cahokia
and other Mississippian centers. Competition
between west Alabama groups escalated into violent
encounters; arrow points and similar wounds are
frequently found on skeletons from this time period.[8]

Under these new conditions, Terminal Woodland

peoples began to borrow Mississippian artifacts and cultural practices. By the 1100s, west Alabama populations were using a mix of Woodland and Mississippian techniques. Some people continued to make their houses and pottery in the Woodland style; others were adopting the Mississippian practices of intensive corn farming, distinctive wall-trench houses, and new pottery styles. Still other groups used a "hybrid" house style that combined the older Terminal Woodland house forms of sunken floors or single-set posts with the new Mississippian wall-trench construction methods;[9] such sites produce both Woodland and Mississippian pottery styles. While competition and trade apparently increased Terminal Woodland peoples' motivation to acquire Mississippian products and ideas, the technical details of house, pottery, and other artifact production would be difficult to acquire from a long distance. For this reason, some archaeologists conclude that Mississippian groups moved into west Alabama, settled among local Terminal Woodland peoples, and soon intermarried.[10] How else can we explain a mix of the local and foreign cultural practices and products used by people living at the same archaeological sites?

The Origins of Moundville

In general terms, archaeologists know what was required to create Moundville: a society divided into families of high and low social rank, and a permanent office of leadership. Archaeologists also confirm that the conditions to form such a society came together once the Mississippian way of life was established in west Alabama: a productive food economy, a growing population, and an increased level of both competition (warfare) and cooperation (alliance and trade) among groups. Precisely how Moundville's society of hereditary social rank and strong leaders originated remains unknown, but there is evidence of both local sources for this cultural change as well as external influence from other Mississippian societies.

Archaeologists who favor local sources of change propose that competition between rival families for power favored those who could provide more food, more goods, and more labor to create feasts, host celebrations, make crafts, and build mounds. Families who could do these things gained more followers and higher status than those who could not. On the other hand, the ideas, products, and organization needed to achieve these goals may have been borrowed from Mississippian settlements elsewhere or brought to west Alabama by Mississippian settlers. It is now clear that all of the Mississippian cultural practices that appeared in west Alabama in the 1100s—intensified corn production, the mound-farmstead settlement organization, distinctive forms of pottery, wall-trench houses—were first implemented at mound centers that had already been flourishing in regions to the north and west for a hundred years. This new way of life would soon sweep aside the last vestiges of local Woodland culture. Once established, Mississippians in west Alabama would chart a distinctive course of regional development and, from their great center of Moundville, make their mark in the larger Mississippian world.

4

"This Great Group of Mounds"

So wrote Clarence B. Moore when he first encountered Moundville. Even the matter-of-fact Moore could not maintain his usual understatement when describing the site. There are other large Mississippian archaeological sites, but few are so well preserved or beautifully composed. With fire, stone axes, and shell hoes, the people of Moundville transformed the forest into a community. Without benefit of wheeled vehicles or draft animals, human muscle power felled thousands of trees and moved countless basket loads of soil. While the massive earthen mounds dominate the landscape, other structures provided shelter and security. This chapter describes mounds and structures, how this built environment met individual needs, and how the site design illustrates the organization and values of the community.

The Environment and Its Bounty

As in other Mississippian towns, the inhabitants of Moundville drew most of their resources from the local environment. The preeminent feature of the environment is the Black Warrior River. Arising in the hilly uplands of the Cumberland Plateau, the river once crossed a series of shallow falls and shoals

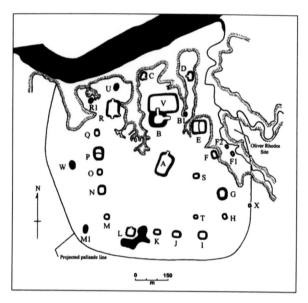

Map of Moundville.

(now inundated by locks and dams) at the fall line where Tuscaloosa is today, fifteen miles north of Moundville. From there the river flows south onto the Gulf Coastal Plain, a physiographic region of broad swampy floodplains and low hills. A subdivision of the coastal plain, known as the "Black Belt," is a zone of prairies, canebrakes, cedar groves, and rich soils that begins a few miles south of Moundville. The waterway connected Moundville and its support population of dispersed small settlements to the diverse plant, animal, and mineral resources of uplands, floodplain, and prairie.

The river was life to Moundville's people. Fertile soil renewed by floods and prepared by burning

Regional map.

away the vegetation nourished corn, the staple crop. Soil worked by hand with stone or shell hoes produced beans, squash, sunflowers, and gourds. From the water came fish and turtles, an important part of the diet. Hardwood trees produced acorns and nuts that supported people and the deer, turkey, and other animals important to the food economy. Without domesticated animals other than the dog, the Moundville Mississippians relied on wild sources of meat.

The regional and local environment satisfied all basic requirements of the Mississippian way of life. Studies of human skeletons from Moundville reveal that people were relatively healthy, although few lived past fifty.[1] Poor sanitation fostered infections, which resulted in high infant mortality. Both arthritis and tuberculosis were present. Tooth decay plagued many as a result of the high carbohydrate content of the corn diet. The environment's bounty and a technology of stone, pottery, wood, shell, cane, and other mineral, plant, and animal products ensured a growing population at the time of Moundville's founding. The site of Moundville was especially favored as a settlement location because it rests on a natural terrace above the highest floods. Just prior to Moundville's growth into a major town, this locale was already heavily settled.[2]

A Tour of Moundville

Gazing out over Moundville's green spaces today, imagine how it looked crowded with people and houses in the year 1250. Standing at the center of the great town, all of Moundville's architectural features would spread out before you: the central plaza, the majestic mounds, the small wood-and-thatch buildings arranged in clusters behind the mounds, the encircling fortifications, and, beyond, fields of corn. Trees would be cleared away. The mounds and plaza would not be green and grass covered but sheathed in the earth tones of smooth, hard clay. Let's take a tour of Moundville.

Artist re-creation of Moundville. (Artwork by Steven Patricia. Also courtesy of the Art Institute of Chicago.)

The Central Plaza

At Mississippian sites plazas are common public spaces. Moundville's central plaza is not a natural level plain but a prehistoric construction project. Limited probes reveal fill dirt deposited three feet deep in some places. The full extent of leveling and filling to create the plaza is unknown, but impressive amounts of labor went into the effort. Artifacts found beneath the fill indicate that plaza and mound construction began around A.D. 1200. We know that people did not live in the central portion of the plaza because the fill deposit and plaza surface are mostly devoid of artifacts; there are few clues about activities here. Presumably people assembled

in the plaza for ceremonial events, ritual proces-
sions, and games. In historic times, various Indian
groups used smaller plazas with central fire pits as
ceremonial "square grounds." Perhaps the historic
square grounds developed from the larger public
plazas of Mississippian times. Smaller, less obvious
plazas may exist at Moundville, but they remain
undetected.

The Mounds

The mounds at Moundville, like those at other Mississippian centers, are a form of monumental architecture. The mounds range from three to fifty-seven
feet high. The mounds are so big that it is difficult
for archaeologists to examine them completely.
While Moore dug into most of the mounds, only
Mounds A, E, F, G, M, P, Q, R, and V have received
more than superficial examination with modern
techniques.[3] Much about the mounds remains
unknown. Still, archaeologists know how and when
most mounds were built, and they have identified
activities that took place on some of the mounds.

Most of the mounds are platforms built in the
shape of steep-sided, flat-topped pyramids with
square or rectangular bases and one or more ramps
for access to the summit. The platform mounds are
composed of successive construction stages of soil
and clay. Each stage summit served as the surface for
wooden buildings and activities until covered over
by the next stage. The size of the labor force and the
number of additions constructed over time deter-

mined the size of mounds. As Moore first discovered, some of the mounds contain human remains,
but others do not. Some high places originally designated as mounds, such as U, W, and M1, are not
constructed mounds at all but gradual accumulations of midden generated by dense concentrations
of houses.[4]

Plan of the Mounds

Like other Mississippian platform mounds, Moundville's mounds are oriented to the cardinal direc-
tions. The likely reason for this is that the Mississippians conceived of a mound as a world symbol, a
representation of the earth in miniature, and thus
properly positioned at the center of the four direc-
tions.[5] Other than this symbolism, there is no convincing evidence that the builders followed any
complex astronomical principles to position the
mounds. Instead, social values guided the plan of
the mounds.

Christopher Peebles first observed that the
arrangement, form, and function of the mounds
provide clues about Moundville's society.[6] Around
the plaza periphery, larger mounds without burials
alternate with smaller mounds that contain human
remains to create pairs of large and small mounds.
Some evidence suggests that larger mounds without
burials were the residences of leaders and high-status
families; smaller mounds contain burials but yield
evidence of ceremonial buildings and other special
activities as well. The second largest mound in vol-

ume, Mound A, occupies the center of the arrangement. To the north, Mound B is the largest and highest mound at the site, flanked by two other large mounds (R, E). The northern portion of the site has the largest mounds (R, B, and E) and the mounds with the most elaborate burials (C, D). Mounds decrease in size from north to south around the plaza. For these reasons, archaeologists conclude that Moundville's highest-ranking families lived in the northern portion of the site.

Peebles concluded that Moundville society was composed of ranked kin groups. Following Peebles's lead, archaeologist Vernon J. Knight proposed that these kin groups, possibly the local members of a clan, each used a pair of large and small mounds around the plaza.[7] Anthropologists define a clan as a group of families that consider themselves related, usually through descent from a common ancestor. Clans impose various rules and obligations on their members that govern marriage, politics, rituals, and other important matters. In the historic Southeast, children inherited membership in their mother's clan.[8] Because clan members were considered related, they could not marry persons of the same clan; spouses were members of separate clans. Southeastern Indian towns were composed of clans with different social ranks. Each clan used a ceremonial structure positioned around the square ground according to social rank. Knight suggests a similar community organization for Moundville, with mounds arranged around the plaza according to the social rank of the clan that used it.[9]

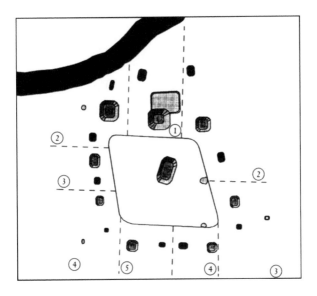

Possible division of mounds by rank: 1 = highest.
Mounds with burials are black.

Different Uses of the Mounds

Mound A is different from the other mounds. Its
unique central location and large size suggest it was
a public monument or place of assembly for the
entire community rather than a clan monument.
The even more impressive Mound B is directly
north of Mound A. Though it was once referred to
as the "Temple Mound," most archaeologists interpret Mound B as the residence of the top-ranking
leader. Early European explorers observed Southeastern chiefs' houses placed on the highest mounds.
In fact, owing to the lack of modern excavation,
there is little direct evidence for the function of
Mound A or Mound B. However, Mound B,

together with residential Mounds R and E, and the high-status burials found in Mounds C and D, appear to form an elite northern precinct separate from the other mounds. It was in Mound C that Moore found the elaborate costumed burials accompanied by the unique copper-bladed axes that Peebles determined were symbols of the highest leadership positions at Moundville.

Excavations by Knight and students at The University of Alabama provide insights into the uses of the paired large and small mounds around the plaza. Knight compared Mound G, a large mound without burials, to Mound Q, a small mound with burials.[10] In the interest of preservation, the two mounds were only partially excavated. Both mounds had many similar characteristics. Both had the remains of buildings on their summits and evidence of food remains mostly consisting of corn, deer, and turkey. However, the mounds show evidence of different activities and uses. Small Mound Q had scattered fragments of human skulls and long bones, a grave pit emptied of its contents in prehistoric times, a wide variety of pottery vessels that had been broken while in use, stone chisels, axes, drills, saws, and other evidence of craft-making, abundant paint pigments, and copper, shell, feather, and other ornaments. These materials suggest that Mound Q was a place where costumes, paints, stone palettes, and other ritual materials were made and used. In contrast, larger Mound G had no human remains and

Excavation at Mound Q. (Courtesy of Office of Archaeological Services, The University of Alabama Museums.)

only low-frequency evidence of the crafting, ornament, or ritual materials found at Mound Q.

Knight interpreted both mounds as elite residences, but there are other possibilities. Mound Q
may have supported a special building devoted to a
clan's rituals and ceremonies, where the clan's sacred
objects were made, stored, and used, and where
food was offered and consumed during religious
rites. The human bones may be ancestral relics or
grisly war trophies. Mound G may have been a clan
leader's house, a meeting place where important clan
members and visitors gathered to eat and drink,[11] or
some combination of these functions. Throughout

the world, societies with clans often had ceremonial clan structures and chiefs' houses that also served as meeting halls. Southeastern Indians used similar buildings in early historic times.

Knight's excavations on Mound V produced an unexpected discovery. The remains of two large square buildings, joined together by a short passageway, were partially uncovered. The wooden buildings form a structure known as an earth lodge, the first one discovered at Moundville. Mississippian earth lodges had soil banked against the outside walls and over the roof. The significance of the discovery lies in the fact that earth lodges are a foreign building tradition at Moundville, introduced from elsewhere late in the history of the site.[12]

Residential Areas

Moundville's wooden buildings rotted away long ago. All that remains are square or rectangular patterns of soil stains left by wall posts and foundation trenches. Several different forms of houses and public buildings went in and out of common use over time. The first occupants built their houses in a style common in Woodland times. Small wall poles were set in postholes or in a sunken floor. A new house form, with wall poles set in trenches, soon replaced the Woodland-style houses. These wall-trench buildings are the most common house form at Moundville. Still later houses changed again, from wall-trench structures to wattle-and-daub buildings with gabled roofs resting on rigid vertical posts set

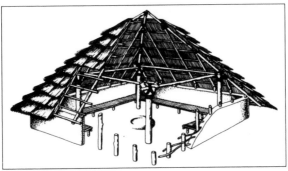

Above: Reconstruction of flexed-pole wall-trench building. (Courtesy of University of Tennessee Press.)

Below: Reconstruction of rigid post wattle-and-daub building. (Courtesy of University of Tennessee Press.)

in postholes. Canes (wattles) were woven between wall posts and covered with a mud-and-straw plaster (daub). Fire hearths were clay-lined basins placed at the center of house floors. Interior postholes suggest that raised beds were sometimes present.

Residential Groups

Most people lived in clusters of five to twenty houses, known as residential groups, arrayed between the
mounds and the palisade line.[13] Each residential
group is a cluster of houses that remains separated
from the next closest group by an empty space. All
residential groups have the same house forms and
range of house sizes. This repetitive community pattern indicates that residential groups probably represent a basic unit of Moundville's social organization,
perhaps a kin group that composed the ranked clans
identified in the mound arrangement. If this was the
case, then it is likely that each kin group's members
lived together in a residential group and that these
people were affiliated with one of the mound pairs
identified by Peebles and Knight. Centrally placed
Mound A does not fit this repetitive spatial pattern
of residential groups and mounds, an additional reason to suspect that it had a communal or public
function.

Superimposed house remains and accumulated
midden reveal that people lived in their residential
groups for decades. Wooden houses decayed after
several years. Residents rebuilt their houses in the
same place. Clearly, it was important to maintain a
house location among one's kin. Most houses were
quite small, with only one room barely large enough
to sleep more than a few people. Some residential
groups had a single building larger than the other
structures in the group, sometimes with two or

more rooms. While most structures in a residential group were dwellings, these larger buildings may have served special purposes, such as sweathouses (a hut for steam baths) or as storehouses for corn and other goods.[14]

Fortifications

A fortified log stockade or palisade protected the plaza, mounds, and residential groups. Visitors to Moundville in the nineteenth century could still see the remnant palisade line as a low embankment encircling the site. To erect the walls, rot-resistant pine posts about one foot in diameter were set upright in trenches as much as seven feet deep. Towers (bastions) that served as platforms for archers defending the walls projected out from the palisade at regular intervals. The projected path of the palisade line around the site is an estimate based on Lupton's 1860s sketch map of the visible remnant and segments uncovered at three locations by excavations in the 1980s and 1990s.[15] If this projected line is accurate, the wall was more than a mile long, a building feat that required thousands of trees to be felled, trimmed, hauled, and set into place. Current evidence indicates that the mound-plaza arrangement and palisade were established at approximately the same time. Palisade repair and rebuilding occurred frequently for about a century. All known palisade segments date to before A.D. 1300; apparently Moundville was unfortified after this date.

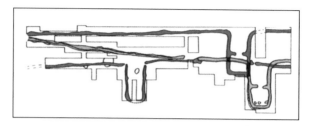

Plan view of Moundville palisade segment with bastions. Colors show segments built at different times. (Courtesy of Joseph O. Vogel.)

5

History Written with a Shovel

In the year 1250 Moundville was a fortified settlement filled with people. A century later, Moundville had changed from a bustling town to a ceremonial center of solemn rituals and funerals. By the time the Europeans arrived in the 1500s, people had mostly abandoned Moundville. The customs, values, and beliefs of Moundville's people varied through time as did the manner in which they built and used their settlement. Through archaeology, it is possible to construct a brief history of Moundville.[1] The names of the people who lived there are unknown, but the materials they left behind document their collective deeds and accomplishments.

First Settlement: A.D. 1120–1200

Although Archaic spear points and Woodland pottery indicate the presence of earlier peoples at Moundville, the oldest substantial occupation began around A.D. 1120. These first settlers lived in small one-room houses dispersed across the natural terrace above the river. It was a time of cultural transition between centuries-old Woodland traditions and the new Mississippian way of life. Increases in corn production provided a food surplus that could support larger populations and new forms of social organization.

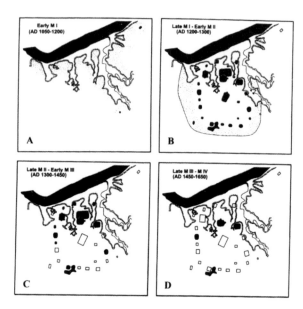

Settlement changes at Moundville: occupied mounds are black, abandoned mounds are open rectangles, domestic occupation area is stippled.

The common Mississippian settlement of dispersed farmsteads arranged around a mound center appears in the region at this time. Some families channeled the surplus food and labor into the construction of the first mounds: Mound X, a low rise near the park entrance, and site 1TU50, a mound located just north of the park. The history and use of these oldest mounds are poorly known.[2] From limited investigations we know that 1TU50 and Mound X were platforms built in stages and contain evidence of buildings, shell-bead making, use of mica, and food consumption. If they were like the better-known mounds at Moundville, these first platforms supported special buildings where leaders hosted ritual and political activities at central places on the landscape. A society more complex than previous cultures in the Black Warrior River valley was now in place. Moundville itself was not yet a large town but a small community of widespread houses whose inhabitants came together for rituals at two small mounds.[3]

Capital Town: A.D. 1200–1300

Around A.D. 1200 a remarkable series of events transformed the Moundville site. As the residential population grew rapidly, an enormous construction project began on the mound-plaza-palisade arrangement. Archaeologists do not know why so many people came to the Moundville site. The construction of the palisade at this time suggests defense may have been a motivation. Also during this time, people stopped using Mound X and the 1TU50 mound. In fact, the palisade line went right over Mound X, leaving part of it exposed outside the wall.[4] Perhaps the people who used Mound X and 1TU50 mound moved inside Moundville's walls. If not, then the Moundville community excluded these people from a prominent position in the new social order.

A move to Moundville offered more than improved defense. By joining the new organization emerging at Moundville, families gained greater access to things they could not acquire as easily while living in smaller groups: more food, exotic stone for tools, shell and copper for ornaments, and a sense of common purpose reinforced by new religious practices. With the new town came new expressions of community identity. The use of Woodland house and pottery styles ended and was replaced by exclusively Mississippian styles as residents conformed to a uniform Moundville culture.

Excavations in two areas along the northwest riverbank, known as the PA and ECB tracts, provide clues that the new social order changed how and where people lived at Moundville.[5] House remains in the PA tract date to the time of first settlement prior to 1200. In this older social order, the PA tract houses were spaced far apart and built in combinations of Woodland and Mississippian forms (single-set post, wall trench, sunken floor). House remains in the ECB tract, clustered close together behind the palisade, date to the time of the new social order. In the ECB tract, people stopped building the older Woodland-style houses. They adopted the new wall-trench style exclusively and repeatedly rebuilt their houses in the same place. In the old social order, people moved locations to build a new house. In the new social order, maintaining the same house location among a group of related families was now important. People at Moundville were forming the residential groups of clustered houses and conforming to the values of a new culture.

Based on the number of house remains found at

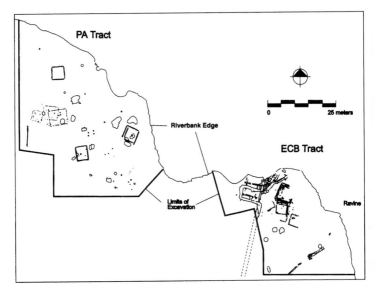

House and palisade remains in the PA and ECB tracts.
(Courtesy of Office of Archaeological Services, The University of Alabama Museums.)

Moundville, perhaps a thousand people lived behind the protective walls.[6] Society consisted of a rank order of individuals and groups. People of high social status were buried in mounds accompanied by ornaments of shell, copper, and stone. Others of lower social status were buried elsewhere with common tools or nothing at all. Moundville was now the center of a complex society with different degrees of social status and rank.

Not everyone in the new social order lived at Moundville. A large portion of Moundville society continued to live in dispersed farmsteads distributed for miles up and down the river valley. Archaeologists have identified two single-mound sites with artifacts in the Moundville style that may date to this time period.[7] The different sizes and types of sites—farmsteads, single-mound centers, and the Moundville multiple-mound center—suggest that a regional political organization had formed. Within a generation, the Moundville site had become the fortified capital town of a political territory.

Ceremonial Center: A.D. 1300–1450

During this period Moundville underwent a radical change from fortified town to sparsely populated ceremonial center. There is evidence that a large portion of the population left Moundville.[8] Maintenance of the palisade ceased; Moundville was apparently without fortifications. The use of Mound A and most mounds in the southern portion of the site ended. People stopped adding new dwellings to the long-established residential groups and moved out. The abandoned residential-group locations became cemeteries. That is, the occupation and rebuilding of houses in these locations ceased, and graves began to accumulate in clustered groupings where the houses had once stood. Perhaps the people buried in these new cemeteries were descendants of the original occupants.[9] In fact, most of the human burials at Moundville date to a time after A.D. 1300, whereas most of the house remains and middens date to earlier times. In other words,

Moundville became a burial place and ceremonial center for people who lived elsewhere.[10]

When people left the great town, where did they go? One clue is the sudden increase in the number of outlying single-mound centers along the river. Both to the north and south of Moundville, at least five new local centers appeared around A.D. 1300, far more than during the previous time period.[11] Each of these local centers had a small resident population surrounded by farmsteads whose families probably came to the local center on a regular basis.

Archaeologists do not know why people moved out of Moundville. One possibility is that wood, game, and good soils became scarce as the population grew. If shortages did occur, however, they were not severe enough to prevent some people from continuing to live at Moundville. Another possible explanation is that the threat of attack by enemies may have diminished, removing the need to live behind a palisade. This explanation is not altogether convincing because other people had always lived at unprotected outlying sites. Yet another possibility is that social divisions in Moundville's society led to conflict that was resolved by groups leaving to establish their own centers. Some archaeologists believe a top-ranked or "paramount chief" and other high-ranking members of society claimed exclusive rights to reside at Moundville and consolidated their power by forcing lower-rank families to move out of the sacred center.[12] Other researchers interpret the move out of Moundville as evidence of a loss of political power by the paramount leader as rival chiefs left with their followers to set up their own mound centers.[13] Whatever the case, Moundville became a place of pilgrimage, ceremonies, and funerals.

Despite the population loss, Moundville was not a vacant ghost town. Mound B and other mounds in the northern part of the site continued to be used. Midden and house remains found near Mounds R and M show that people continued to live in other areas of the site. Differences in the contents and placement of graves are evidence that degrees in social status and rank continued to be present in Moundville society. During this interval, pottery vessels and ornaments of stone, copper, and shell were decorated with symbols such as cross-in-circle, hand-and-eye, forked eye, falcons, winged serpents, skulls and bones, scalps, and arrows. The precise meanings of the symbols are unknown, but historic Southeastern Indian beliefs provide some clues. Archaeologists interpret the symbols as an expression of Moundville society's concerns with ancestors, mythological beings, war, and death.

Decline and Abandonment: A.D. 1450–1650

Moundville underwent a gradual decline as a ceremonial center. Although Moundville continued to be the scene of funerals, the number of burials decreased. The dead no longer received the copper, shell, and stone ornaments of high rank. Production of the striking symbols that had held such powerful meanings for Moundville's people came to an end.[14]

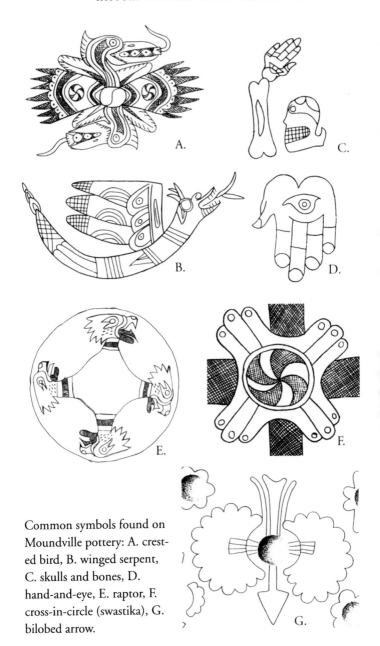

Common symbols found on Moundville pottery: A. crested bird, B. winged serpent, C. skulls and bones, D. hand-and-eye, E. raptor, F. cross-in-circle (swastika), G. bilobed arrow.

Most mounds were no longer in use by the mid-1500s. Only Mounds B, E, P, and V have evidence of mound-top activities, and mound construction ceased entirely.[15] One late addition to Moundville's buildings was the earth lodge constructed on Mound V. Some archaeologists interpret earth lodges as council houses. Perhaps the appearance of this new form of public building signals a shift in leadership from hereditary chiefs to a governing council.[16]

The reasons for Moundville's decline remain unknown. At least six outlying single-mound centers continued to be important places during this time period.[17] These local centers gained a greater following even as Moundville continued to lose regional influence. Some people were buried at local mound centers during this time; perhaps burial at Moundville was no longer as highly valued as it had once been. Long periods of drought occurred in some areas of the Southeast in the 1400s, but researchers have not yet identified ancient droughts in the Moundville region.[18] If droughts at Moundville did lead to the loss of the corn crop, people may have left in search of new lands. Whatever the cause of decline, the old religious symbols and markers of high status were gone. Moundville was no longer an important political or ceremonial place.

More changes swept the region when Spanish explorer Hernando De Soto and his army entered the vicinity of Moundville in 1540. The army passed through small villages, but the Spanish accounts make no mention of a site that could have been Moundville. Population levels fell in the valley, probably as a result of the impact of diseases introduced through European contact. At small sites in the Moundville region and elsewhere in Alabama, the custom of placing a person's bones in large pots or "burial urns" became widespread. Evidence from skeletons indicates poor health and nutrition.[19] Pottery and other artifacts show little of the decoration, diversity of shapes, or skill of previous times. Moundville has yielded up only a few burial urns, perhaps left there as reverential offerings to the faded glory of a sacred place. Moundville was abandoned by 1600, if not before. Soon thereafter, the Black Warrior River valley became an uninhabited borderland between the Creeks to the east and the Choctaws to the west.

De Soto encounters the Indians of Alabama. (Courtesy of Riverhill Enterprises.)

Moundville Timeline

Date	Period	Phase
1650		
1540		
1520	Protohistoric	Moundville IV
1450		
1400	Late Mississippi	Moundville III
1350		
1300		
1260		Moundville II
1200	Middle Mississippi	
1175		
1120	Early Mississippi	Moundville I
1100		
1020	Terminal Woodland	West Jefferson
900		
800		Carthage
700	Late Woodland	

Regional Developments	World Events
Region depopulated	
Villages with burial urns	Trial of Galileo
	Jamestown founded
De Soto's army	
	Height of Inca Empire
Mound V earth lodge	First Voyage of Columbus
Most mounds abandoned	
Burial at Moundville decreases	
	Italian Renaissance
Residential population decreases	
Burial at Moundville increases	Ming Dynasty begins
Many mounds abandoned	Hopi towns founded
Palisade abandoned	Travels of Marco Polo
Residential population increases	Magna Carta
Mounds, plaza, and palisade established	Mongol Empire expands
	Crusades
	Notre Dame cathedral
First mounds built	construction begins
	Chaco Canyon climax
Regional population increases	Norman conquest of England
Corn production intensifies	
Small sites	Classic Maya collapse
Introduction of the bow	

6

Life and Death at Moundville

What was it like to live at ancient Moundville? How can we understand a way of life so different from ours today? Maybe the gap of time and
experience between them and us is just too great.
Unlike recent histories populated with named and
knowable figures, the men and women of ancient
Moundville remain anonymous. Without written
records, all we have are the physical remains.
Ancient customs, values, and beliefs do not become
fossils we can dig up and examine. The remains are
fragmented and partially preserved, so our knowledge of a prehistoric culture comes to us in bits and
pieces. Much about prehistory will always remain a
mystery, but we can still learn from the past, even if
the story is incomplete. Archaeologists can discover
relationships between the artifacts and other materials that reveal parts of the whole culture and many
past activities. What is most remarkable about
Moundville archaeology is not that we know so little
but that we have learned so much.

Moundville Archaeology

To learn more about how archaeologists piece
together the Moundville story, let us look over the
shoulder of three archaeologists as they gather evi-

dence and draw conclusions about one place at the Moundville site. The following section presents a "you are there" reconstruction of actual events. As a retelling of the past, these historical sketches rely on informed imagination, but the individual archaeologists are real people. Existing records are the sources for the description of the excavation and the discoveries made there. In the sketches, each of the archaeologists has a different perspective as they interpret the same evidence at three different times—1939, 1969, and 2003.

Mound State Monument, 1939

Maurice Goldsmith, archaeologist, is supervising his crew of "CCC boys" as they dig in the path of the newly paved road that will circle the park. The men work hard in the hot sun. Many are illiterate, so Goldsmith takes the notes. To record the horizontal provenience of finds, the excavation block is marked off in 5' x 5' squares, each designated by a coordinate. Watching the men dig, Goldsmith is satisfied with the results. In a deposit that is only three feet deep, soil stains outline the remains of an 18' x 26' wall-trench house, designated Structure 8 (S-8). In and around the house are a dozen burials in the shallow grave pits typical of Moundville.[1] There are plenty of artifacts, too. Besides potsherds, which Goldsmith does not even glance at anymore, S-8 has yielded two well-made bowls, two effigy pot handles, red and green paint lumps, a rare bit of rock crystal, and three stone discoidals, one so crude it

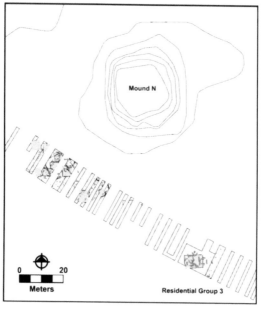

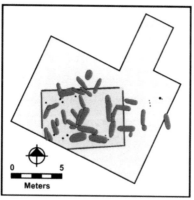

Above: Location of Residential Group 3 at Moundville. (Courtesy of Gregory D. Wilson.)

Below: Plan view of Structure 8, Residential Group 3, showing house outline and burials. (Courtesy of Gregory D. Wilson.)

A stone discoidal.
Diameter 6 cm.
(Courtesy of The
University of Ala-
bama Museums.)

must have been incomplete when it was thrown away.

The graves contain the poorly preserved remains of men, women, children, and infants. Burial goods found thus far include an engraved stone disk placed under the skull of an adult, several wide-mouth pottery bottles, fish and frog effigy bowls, a copper ear spool, and pottery disks thought to be game pieces or spindle whorls. When the ancient people tried to place graves close together they sometimes dug into earlier graves; many of the skeletons lack a hand or foot.[2] Goldsmith ambles over to the excavation where a board holds artifacts shoveled up that morning. On the board are three copper fishhooks, bright green with corrosion.

"Mr. Goldsmith! Take a look at this!" He walks over to where the men are uncovering another burial from graves dug into and below S-8. Goldsmith gazes down at a poorly preserved adult skeleton in a shallow grave. The body lies extended on the back, head to the east. "This is Burial 2748. Only about

A frog effigy pottery bowl. Height 11.5 cm. (Courtesy of The University of Alabama Museums.)

five feet tall," says Goldsmith, "probably a woman." A wide-mouth pottery bottle, dark in color, rests at the skull. The worker points at an object by the skeleton's right knee. Goldsmith bends down for a closer look at an oblong pendant, ground from a red stone. Incised on the upper part of the pendant is a cross-in-circle design. Below that is an incised hand-and-eye image.

Goldsmith walks back to his field desk. He carefully checks the numbered sheet for the burial. There is more to record now that Mr. DeJarnette has sent down the new form TVA 2097 from the big digs going on up north.[3] For each burial, Goldsmith has recorded the artifacts found in the grave and the depth of the grave below ground surface. He has noted whether the burial is "intrusive," meaning the grave pit was dug down from one of the four levels

Oblong stone pendant
incised with cross-in-circle
and hand-in-eye image.
Length 4.6 cm. (Courtesy of
The University of Alabama
Museums.)

or layers of the deposit, or "precedent," designating
that the grave originated in the lowest level. At first,
Goldsmith was puzzled about the depth-and-level
information. If there was more than one culture
here, stacked up in layers, he could see the need to
sort them out by depth. However, all the burials
belong to the Moundville culture. Still, the sequence
of burials from top to bottom might prove useful
somehow. Now he carefully matches Burial 2748 to
the level from which it originated, as he has done
with the others. "Ready!" shouts one of the workers.
"Time to draw the burial," he thinks as he rises from
his seat, "and maybe take a photograph after lunch."

Florida Atlantic University, 1969

Anthropology graduate student Christopher Peebles sits in his campus office. On the desk before him is a master map he has drawn of all excavations at Moundville.[4] The map has taken weeks of work. Today Peebles is writing up a description of the 1939 Roadway excavation block, coordinates 15+00 to 15+50. "Good thing Goldsmith used the TVA form on this block," he muses. Now it is possible to understand the order of events. Goldsmith recognized four levels or layers of soil in the deposit. The lowest and oldest one, level 4, contained eleven burials. Later, wall-trench building S-8 was built at the top of level 3. This is where Goldsmith found the bowls, effigies, paint, and discoidals, he notes. Peebles begins to tap his typewriter keys. "The third earliest level, level 2, not only contained the majority of burials (burials intruded from level 1) but it was also the level from which the burials in level 3 were intruded."[5] He stops and thinks, "So people lived in S-8 and buried some of their family under the floor—not unusual—but then after S-8 was abandoned and covered by level 1, people came back to this spot and dug more graves there. Why? How did they know where to return if the building was gone? How many years separated these events? Too bad the CCC archaeologists did not have radiocarbon dating, or keep plant remains, or craft production debris, or animals bones, or. . . ." He glances at his watch and leaves to teach a class.

University of North Carolina, 2003

Anthropology graduate student Gregory Wilson sits in front of his computer. From Peebles's work, he has made digital maps of all the Roadway excavation structures, burials, fire basins, postholes, and other features. Using the sophisticated Geographic Information System (GIS), he has created "layers" or overlay digital maps of archaeological features from different time periods. Wilson has something else that was unavailable to Peebles: an accurate method for dating the archaeological finds. Wilson looks at the Roadway block he calls Residential Group 3, one of twelve such groups of houses and burials he is studying. "It is the same pattern again," he reflects. The Roadway houses date to A.D. 1200–1300, but most of the burials at the residential groups date to after the abandonment of the houses, from A.D. 1300–1450. Residential Group 3 just confirms again that Dr. Steponaitis's interpretation of the Moundville site history is correct.[6] For some reason, Moundville underwent a transformation from a fortified town to a depopulated ceremonial center. At the ceremonial center, people came to bury their dead at the places where the old houses once stood. As Wilson turns off the computer, he considers once again what this pattern may mean: "These later funerals must have been for people who believed that they had some longtime relationship to the people who had lived in the houses. Perhaps they were the descendants of the house residents."[7]

Putting Flesh on the Skeletons

Each of these archaeologists applied the skills and methods available to explore ancient Moundville. Knowledge accumulated with each decade, and some older methods and practices have ceased. For example, archaeologists no longer excavate graves at Moundville because some American Indian peoples consider it disrespectful of the dead. At this protected site, there is no need to disturb burials; the record of graves found long ago continues to produce new information, as archaeology is about more than just finding bones and artifacts. The records and objects of Residential Group 3 tell us about ancient life—as well as death—at Moundville. What follows is an interpretation of events at Residential Group 3, told as a story. It is an exercise in imagination, but other than the names, emotions, and personalities, the information in the story comes from archaeology at Moundville, with a sprinkling of clues from the customs of early historic Southeastern Indians. There is no guarantee that this story is accurate. Nevertheless, as we observed earlier, stones, bones, and soil stains do not speak, so if we want to know more about the people than a dull inventory of dusty things left behind, we must interpret in a knowledgeable way that is consistent with the evidence.[8] Now with our props of artifacts and features identified, we can arrange them on our prehistoric stage and present a play of ancient Moundville, in two acts.

Act I: Life in a Fortified Town

The time: our year A.D. 1270, June; their year of the late flood, fourth summer of Great Sun Serpent Sting, Blackberry Moon.

The place: our S-8, Residential Group 3, Moundville; their House of White-Wind Mother, her husband, Bear Paw, and their daughter, Hummingbird-girl.

The scene: the house interior. Bear Paw, a man in his forties, sits grinding a stone discoidal with a block of sandstone. White-Wind Mother, age thirty-six, stands crushing burnt mussel shell with a wooden mortar and pestle.[9]

Bear Paw pauses in his work and looks around him. He is content this night. Cane mats cover the walls and floors of the house, which soften the noise of distant drums. The robes he sits upon cushion his leg, so there is no pain from his healing wound. White-Wind Mother has her jars, bowls, baskets, gourds, bags, bundles, and other woman-stuff arrayed along one wall. Very little in the house is his, except some cold season garments White-Wind Mother has in a basket somewhere and a pair of leggings she is mending. His weapons hang in his clan house across the plaza, where no child or woman can touch them. Not that he is likely to use them again, he reflects. He glances at his wife. Having poured the shell particles into a bowl, White-Wind Mother lays aside her potting tools.

"It will rain tomorrow," he says to her.

"No, I think not."

"Then why are you stopping your pot magic?"

"Do you not hear the drums? I wish to see the celebrated beauty they bring for the Great Sun. They say she is bewitched."

"Nonsense, people squawk like jays."

"Yes, they do, and they will squawk if you do not go."

"I will finish this stone."

"Stones! Ha! Ha!"

Without stopping his grinding, Bear Paw exclaims, "Woman! Important people speak of my game stones with admiration the length and breadth of this aged river. My stones have a place of honor among the trophies of all the clan houses."

"All the clan houses?" she teases. "Ha!"

Suddenly, Hummingbird-girl, age seventeen, bursts into the room. Clad in white doeskin, she has cornmeal dots painted across her face. Two wooden disks, white with red spirals, adorn her ears.

"Father! Mother! The procession is coming through the palisade gate!"

In her excitement, she spins around in a circle. *Always flitting hither and yon, like her namesake,* thinks Bear Paw.

"Your father's not going," announces White-Wind Mother.

"But Father, we must all go see the wonder!" gasps the girl.

Bear Paw speaks. "Why are you wearing your fine apparel? It is not you who will be married this eve."

Bride of the Great Sun. (Courtesy of The University of Alabama Museums.)

"Everyone will be there!" whines the girl, stamping her foot.

Hmmm, disrespectful of her father, he observes. She has the fierce spirit of the tiny bird, the first thing he saw the day of her naming. Bear Paw continues to grind the disk and says, "You say everyone, but you mean him. Is it not so?"

"Truly it is so, Father."

Without looking up, Bear Paw says, "You need not go."

"Why not!" sniffs Hummingbird, tearing up. "Why do you not like him? Is it because he is not of your clan?"

More disrespect, he reflects. He must let her go to have some peace in his wife's house.[10] "Because he is among us now," says Bear Paw as he shoots a glance at the slit-like door in the corner.

Hummingbird whirls around, runs to the door, and stops. Her hand flies to her mouth. Beyond the door, a figure stands motionless, backlit by the dying sun. *This is not him,* she thinks. *No, no . . . it is him, but different!* The young man's eyes are bloodshot but as alert as a falcon's. A painted red hand covers one part of his face. Black paint stains his teeth and lips. His left hand is entirely red. Over his left breast is a new sun tattoo, swollen and bloody. From his red sash protrudes a war club, painted in the image of the Master Woodpecker's head, the ochre-smeared stone blade serving as the bird's beak. The man wears his hair twisted in the shell-beaded forelock of the warrior. He stares right through Hummingbird, toward Bear Paw. Slowly, the warrior raises his hand to his forehead, then holds it outstretched, palm out. On his white-painted palm is the image of an eye. Bear Paw returns a casual version of the warrior's salute and then resumes grinding.

"Oak Leaf?" asks Hummingbird, using the boy-name of her suitor. "Is it you?"

"No!" the warrior shouts. "That one is no more! It is I, Left-Hand Killer!"

White-Wind Mother's face grows serious, while Hummingbird stares wide-eyed, transfixed by the warrior's fearsome visage. Bear Paw wonders if the boy is going to shout his new name at everyone he encounters for the next several moons. He had seen the return of the war party earlier in the day, but Hummingbird and White-Wind Mother had been absent, gone to the clan field.

Left-Hand Killer makes a sudden motion and a hide-wrapped package hits the ground at the doorway. With a shriek of delight, the girl darts forward, grabs the package, and turns to display the venison shoulder, first to her father, then to her mother.

I knew it would come to pass, ponders Bear Paw. *At least I will eat well on the new day. Perhaps White-Wind Mother will rub the meat with salt and leeks, and . . .*

"Father?" says Hummingbird. Bear Paw stops grinding. He puts the stone behind him but, unnoticed in the dark, it rolls into a crack in the dirt floor by the wall and is lost. Bear Paw hesitates a moment, and then says the customary words his daughter longs to hear: "It is the house of my wife."

Now Hummingbird turns to her mother, breathless. The warrior beyond the door neither moves nor speaks. White-Wind Mother leans forward, puts her hand on the oozing chunk, and gives the ancient blessing: "Meat is in my house, and so it will be in the house of my daughter."[11]

"Mother!" squeals the girl as she touches her mother's feet, twirls around, and races out the door, only to return a second later to wave a hand at her father's feet. Then she is gone. Beyond the door, all is blackness.

The man and his wife sit for a long time, saying nothing. The drums in the plaza grow louder.

Presently, Bear Paw sighs and says, "Then it is done."

"Yes," says his wife. "There will be the Balancing and Gifting."

"What will your brother Red-Wind Uncle say of this?"

"He approves of the marriage."[12]

Bear Paw raises an eyebrow. "So you knew all along it would be so," he exclaims in a mock indignant tone.

"Of course," she smiles, and begins to sing softly,

> The acorn falls from the tree, the bird leaves the nest.
>
> The acorn falls from the tree, the bird leaves the nest.

The acorn falls from the tree, the bird leaves the nest.

Under the All-Seeing Eye.

Act II: Death in a Ceremonial Center

The time: our year A.D. 1335, March; their year of the big hailstones, eighth winter of Great Sun Panther Tooth, Wind Moon.

The place: our Residential Group 3, after the abandonment of S-8; for them it is the burial ground of White-Wind Grandmother's lineage.

The scene: In the cold hour before dawn, two people stand on a low rise of hard, bare ground. White-Wind Grandmother, a blind woman so old no one knows her age, leans on a staff. Pine Cone–boy, age eight, supports her other arm. Fifty strides to the south, torches light up the Earth-Navel of the Wind Clan House, our Mound M.

"Here," says Pine Cone as he puts his great-great-grandmother's claw-like hand on a red-and-white painted pole protruding from the ground to the height of two men.[13] The feel of the pole causes White-Wind Grandmother to smile. A warm sensation fills her. Now the ancestor's shadow-sides are all about her: her mother, her aunts and uncles, her own daughters. Suddenly, the image of a house comes to her. She hears a voice say, "Hummingbird."[14]

Pine Cone fidgets beside her. His feet are cold. The old woman has stood there now for some time, muttering in low tones at the pole. Pine Cone studies the prayer bowl he is holding. Bright red, white, and yellow paint covers the vessel. In the bowl are little packets wrapped in dried cornhusk, offerings for the ancestor spirits. Something in the bowl glistens in the low light from the sputtering torch behind them. The boy starts to poke his finger at it, but stops to look at White-Wind Grandmother. Sometimes she can see things, somehow. The old woman continues to stare with sightless eyes at the pole, a toothless grin across her face. Just as Pine Cone begins to pick at the prayer bowl contents, he notices the funeral procession has descended from the mound and is now approaching.

"Holy Grandmother," he whispers. The old woman does not move. "Holy Grandmother!" he repeats louder, tugging her robe. "They come now!"

She motions toward the base of the pole. "Put the prayer bowl here, child." Having done so, Pine Cone leads her back several strides to the empty open grave, dug the previous day. Out of the gloom comes the funeral procession moving in single file toward them.

Pine Cone relays the scene to his great-great-grandmother. "Buzzard Claw, the man of medicine, walks ahead. Then there comes Turtle Shell, Master of Ceremonies of Wind Clan. Next there comes tall Bow String, leading four men who carry her on a cedar litter. Now comes Blow Gourd, Guardian of Wind Clan House," referring to the feeble-minded one who lives at the clan house as caretaker. "Behind come many people."

Painted pottery "prayer bowl." Height 17.7 cm. (Courtesy of The University of Alabama Museums.)

"Who is on the litter, child?"

"Why, it is Aunt Swan Wing, wife of Bow String. Do you not remember?"

"Oh, yes, I remember."

"Holy Grandmother?"

"Yes?"

"Why did Buzzard Claw paint a hand-and-eye on Aunt Swan Wing's forehead?"

"Child, this night Swan Wing's soul will depart on the Path of the Souls. She will journey to the Sky World as she walks along the back of the Great Serpent to the place we call The Hand. There in The Hand, her soul will leap through the light portal, which is the Night-Eye of the Creator, just as the Sun is the Day-Eye. It is a difficult journey, so Buzzard Claw has given this blessing of the Hand-and-Eye medicine to guide her on her way. This is why the soul must begin the journey at night."[15] The old woman gestures above her. Pine Cone looks up. The stars are hidden behind a gray curtain of clouds.

Bow String moves forward, deep in his own thoughts. Never in his thirty-eight winters has he felt so drained of the life force, like a man of stone. The long Night of the Crying in the clan house had passed as a blur and now was over. He had sung the Mourning Songs with the others and smeared his face with hot ashes as expected, but it was as if someone else was there in his place. He finds himself standing at the grave. By custom, mourners must leave their grief behind in the clan house, so all stand quietly. Only Buzzard Claw breaks the silence. He twists and gibbers about, slinging medicines, now at the grave, now at the small gathering, now up into the overcast night sky.

A light, cold rain begins to fall. The torchlight flickers over Swan Wing's face, uncovered by the cloth that wraps her. Bow String stares at her, searching for something, but her eyes are as lifeless as pebbles behind the half-closed lids. He had borne more pain than most men had. He had gone without food or water. He had run many steps without stopping. He had suffered wounds in battle. *This grief will be the arrow that kills me,* he thinks, *for her passing is a mortal blow. I am truly alone now without her. No other one knows me.*

A shaman speaks to the heavens. (Courtesy of The University of Alabama Museums.)

The four litter bearers lift Swan Wing's stiff body and lower her into the grave. She lies on her back, head to the east, facing west. Buzzard Claw sprinkles medicine from a pottery bottle over her body and then places it in the grave by her head. A new wave of grief washes over Bow String. He looks up at the sky. *I cannot see the Great Serpent! I cannot see The Hand or the Night-Eye portal! All is gray cloud!* Now a terrible thought comes to him. *How will Swan Wing find the Path of the Souls in all the clouds? What if she loses her way?* Under his robe, he touches the red stone pendant that bears the incised hand-and-eye image. As Buzzard Claw moves away from the grave, Bow String's eyes fall on Swan Wing's face. *Her face!* The rain is washing away the hand-and-eye painted on her forehead. As he watches, the paint dissolves into rivulets that run down her cheeks. Now the four litter bearers are raking dirt over her. Panic seizes Bow String. *She has no guide! She will lose her way! He will never see her again!*

"No!" yells Bow String as he lurches forward. In one swift motion he tears the pendant from his neck and flings it into the grave. It strikes her clothing and slides to rest by her right knee. All eyes are on him now. Bow String hears someone say, "Come, Brother." Gentle arms lead him away from the burial ground. One by one, the mourners come to White-Wind Grandmother, touch her feet in respect, and then melt away into the night. Buzzard Claw kneels, staring at the pendant in the grave for a long time. Suddenly, he signals the four litter bearers and earth spills into the grave, covering the pendant, the bottle, and Swan Wing.

Bow String stands alone in the cold as the last mourner departs. A red-ochre streak of color lights the eastern horizon. Slowly, he turns around and looks upward. The rain has stopped. As he watches, the clouds race by, uncovering the black bowl of the Sky World, adorned by the twinkling Path of the Souls.

7

Visiting Moundville
Archaeological Park

Moundville Archaeological Park preserves
the 320-acre archaeological site of Moundville.
Owned and administered by The University of Alabama, the park offers visitors a unique opportunity
to learn more about the lives of the people who once
called this place home. Protecting one of the largest
and best-preserved archaeological sites in the nation,
Moundville Archaeological Park is on the National
Register of Historic Places. Visited by more than
40,000 people every year, the park has something
for everyone.

Park Features

Many people who come to Moundville Archaeological Park see these important park features, which are
numbered on the visitor map.

1. *Orientation Building.* Located at the park
entrance, this building serves as the park visitor
center. An orientation theater shows an introduc-
tory film about Moundville.

2. *The David L. DeJarnette Archaeological
Research Center.* This research facility is a regional
leader in cultural resource management. The

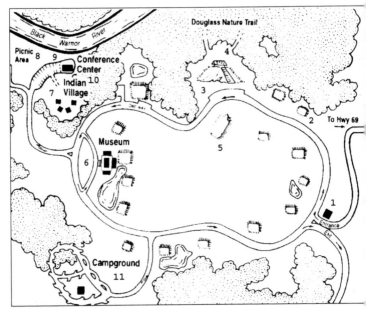

Visitor map of Moundville Archaeological Park. (Courtesy of The University of Alabama Museums.)

12,000-square-foot center consists of an archaeological laboratory, a curation laboratory, and an office complex. The Erskine Ramsey Archaeological Repository stores more than two million artifacts from a dozen states. (The center is not open to the public except by appointment.)

3. *Mound B.* Visitors gain a dramatic overview of the site from the top of fifty-seven-foot-tall Mound B, the highest mound at the site.

4. *Douglass Nature Trail.* This easy, half-mile walk follows a pleasant route through woods, along river bluffs, and past mounds.

5. *Mound A.* Centrally located Mound A is the second largest mound by volume.

6. *The Jones Archaeological Museum.* The Civilian Conservation Corps built the museum in 1939. Ancient Moundville symbols decorate the exterior panels on the Art Deco–style building. Inside, artifacts and exhibits interpret prehistoric life as revealed by more than one hundred years of archaeological investigations. The museum gift shop offers Native American art and crafts, as well as books and videos.

7. *Indian Village.* Visitors can view five reconstructions of ancient houses. Each house contains life-size figures that depict scenes of daily life as reconstructed from archaeological evidence.

8. *Riverbank Overlook.* From this vantage point, visitors have sweeping views of the Black Warrior River. This location was the termination point for the mile-long palisade. Remains of wall segments and tower bastions were found nearby.

9. *Conference Center.* The Nelson B. Jones Conference Center regularly hosts presentations, events, and receptions for private and public groups.

10. *Craft Pavilion.* The John and Delia Roberts Craft Pavilion provides a setting where native artisans demonstrate traditional skills such as pottery making and stone knapping during regularly scheduled showings.

11. *Campground.* Thirty RV and primitive campsites are available for overnight stays. Facilities include water, electricity, and a bathhouse.

Above: Jones Museum. (Courtesy of The University of Alabama Museums.)

Below: Curator at DeJarnette Research Center. (Courtesy of The University of Alabama Museums.)

Programs and Events

   * *Moundville Native American Festival.* Every October members of various tribes, hundreds of Alabama schoolchildren, and visitors from all over arrive for this four-day festival. Visitors can watch native artisans produce pottery and baskets, see demonstrations in the use of bow and arrow, blowgun, and spear-thrower, and participate in native dances. The Children's Area allows kids to make crafts and play traditional games. The Native American Stage features well-known native storytellers, musicians, and dancers. A Living History Camp features costumed participants as they reenact traditional daily practices. Visitors can purchase original works directly from the artist at the Arts Market or sample Native American treats at the food court.

   * *Scheduled Events.* A scheduled series of events and programs such as artists' displays, stickball games, and other attractions occur at the park throughout the year. The Moundville Knap-In takes place in the spring and attracts skilled makers of stone arrow and spear points from all over the United States. Watch as a flint knapper transforms a lump of stone into a functioning tool and a work of art. In the summer, children have fun in a variety of creative and educational activities at the Indian Summer Day Camp. Call the park or visit the park Web site for the schedule of activities.

Living history reenactor, Moundville Native American Festival. (Courtesy of The University of Alabama Museums.)

    * *Archaeological Excavations.* There is no set schedule of excavations. In general, University of Alabama archaeologists and students conduct excavations on weekday afternoons in the fall. Excavations are small-scale, low-impact efforts designed to answer research questions while preserving the remains for future generations. Contact park personnel about ongoing excavations. Visitors are welcome to view the work.

Contact and Visitor Information

* *Location.* Moundville Archaeological Park is located 14 miles south of Tuscaloosa, Alabama, on Highway 69 South. From Interstate I-20/59 take exit 71A and proceed 13 miles south. The park entrance will be located on your right on Highway 69.

* *Park Hours.* The park is open daily from 8:00 a.m. to 8:00 p.m., year-round. The museum is open from 9:00 a.m. to 5:00 p.m.

* *Contact.* For more information, call 205-371-2234. E-mail address is moundville@bama.ua.edu. The Moundville Archaeological Park Web site is http://museums.ua.edu/moundville/guide.html.

Notes

Chapter 1

1. The only exception is the Vikings, who established a short-lived colony on Newfoundland about A.D. 1000. They had no detectable impact on native populations elsewhere in the New World.

Chapter 2

1. Thomas Maxwell, "Tuskaloosa, the Origin of Its Name, Its History, Etc." (paper read before the Alabama Historical Society, 1876), Hoole Library Alabama Collection, University of Alabama.

2. Ibid.

3. Two entertaining sources for this era of American archaeology are Robert Wauchope, *Lost Tribes and Sunken Continents: Myth and Method in the Study of American Indians* (Chicago: University of Chicago Press, 1962); and Robert Silverberg, *Mound Builders of Ancient America: The Archaeology of a Myth* (Greenwich, CT: New York Graphic Society, 1968).

4. Vincas P. Steponaitis, "The Smithsonian Institution's Investigations at Moundville in 1869 and 1882," *Mid-Continental Journal of Archaeology* 8, no. 1 (1983): 127–69.

5. Ibid.

6. Biographical sources for Moore include Lawrence E. Aten and Jerald T. Milanich, "Clarence Bloomfield Moore: A Philadelphia Archaeologist in the Southeastern

United States," in *Philadelphia and the Development of Americanist Archaeology,* ed. Don D. Fowler and David R. Wilcox (Tuscaloosa: University of Alabama Press, 2003), 113–33; H. Newell Wardle, "Clarence Bloomfield Moore (1852–1936)," *Bulletin of the Philadelphia Anthropological Society* 9, no. 2 (1956): 9–11; Vernon James Knight, Jr., "Introduction: The Expeditions of Clarence B. Moore to Moundville in 1905 and 1906," in *The Moundville Expeditions of Clarence Bloomfield Moore,* ed. Vernon James Knight, Jr. (Tuscaloosa: University of Alabama Press, 1996), 1–20.

7. Accessible facsimiles of Moore's Moundville reports are reprinted in *The Moundville Expeditions of Clarence Bloomfield Moore,* ed. Knight.

8. H. Newell Wardle, "The Treasures of Prehistoric Moundville," *Harper's Monthly* 112 (1906): 200–210.

9. Knight, "Introduction."

10. Gregory A. Waselkov, "A History of the Alabama Anthropological Society," *Southeastern Archaeology* 13, no. 1 (1994): 64–76.

11. John A. Walthall, *Prehistoric Indians of the Southeast: Archaeology of Alabama and the Middle South* (Tuscaloosa: University of Alabama Press, 1980), 211–12.

12. Walter B. Jones, "The Indian Mounds at Moundville, Tuscaloosa County" (paper presented to the Board of Regents, Alabama Museum of Natural History, University of Alabama, 1929), on file at the Office of Archaeological Research, Moundville Archaeological Park.

13. Knight, "Introduction."

14. Moundville is located in the same county depicted in the classic document of Depression poverty, James Agee and Walker Evans, *Let Us Now Praise Famous Men*

(Boston: Houghton Mifflin, 1941).

15. Joy D. Baklanoff and Arthur F. Howington, *The Mounds Awaken: Mound State Monument and the Civilian Conservation Corps,* Alabama Museum of Natural History Special Publications No. 3, 1989.

16. Lona Mae Wilson and Jan Whyllson, *Behind the Mounds* (Moundville, AL: Moundville United Methodist Church, 1995).

17. Walthall, *Prehistoric Indians of the Southeast.*

18. Ibid.

19. For biographical sketches of DeJarnette, see Walthall, *Prehistoric Indians of the Southeast,* and Vernon James Knight, Jr., "David Lloyd DeJarnette: 1907–1991," *American Antiquity* 58, no. 4 (1993): 622–25.

20. Wilson and Whyllson, *Behind the Mounds;* Chen-Hsin Lo, "Ritual and Community in a Southern Town" (M.A. thesis, University of Alabama, 1988).

21. Anonymous, quoted in Wilson and Whyllson, *Behind the Mounds.*

22. Christopher S. Peebles, "Excavations at Moundville, 1905–1951" (unpublished manuscript, 1973), on file at the Office of Archaeological Research, Moundville Archaeological Park.

23. Ibid.

24. Christopher S. Peebles, "Moundville: The Social Organization of a Prehistoric Community and Culture" (Ph.D. diss., University of California, Santa Barbara, 1974).

25. Vincas P. Steponaitis, *Ceramics, Chronology, and Community Patterns: An Archaeological Study at Moundville* (New York: Academic Press, 1983).

26. C. Margaret Scarry, "Changes in Plant Production

and Procurement during the Emergence of the Moundville Chiefdom" (Ph.D. diss., University of Michigan, 1986).

27. Mary Lucas Powell, *Status and Health in Prehistory: A Case Study of the Moundville Chiefdom* (Washington, DC: Smithsonian Institution Press, 1988).

28. Paul D. Welch, *Moundville's Economy* (Tuscaloosa: University of Alabama Press, 1991).

Chapter 3

1. A good introduction to Eastern Woodlands prehistory is George R. Milner, *The Moundbuilders: Ancient Peoples of Eastern North America* (London: Thames and Hudson, 2004).

2. John E. Kelley, "The Nature and Context of Emergent Mississippian Cultural Dynamics in the American Bottom," in *Late Woodland Societies: Tradition and Transformation across the Midcontinent,* ed. Thomas E. Emerson, Dale L. McElrath, and Andrew C. Fortier (Lincoln: University of Nebraska Press, 2000), 163–78.

3. Timothy R. Pauketat, *Ancient Cahokia and the Mississippians* (Cambridge: Cambridge University Press, 2004).

4. A readable treatment of the early Spanish–Southeastern Indian encounter is Charles M. Hudson, *Knights of Spain, Warriors of the Sun: Hernando de Soto and the South's Ancient Chiefdoms* (Athens: University of Georgia Press, 1997).

5. A good introduction to the social organization, customs, and beliefs of historic Southeastern Indians is Charles M. Hudson, *The Southeastern Indians* (Knoxville: University of Tennessee Press, 1976).

6. The exception to these generalizations may be the

massive Cahokia site. Archaeologists do not agree about Cahokia's social organization.

7. Ned J. Jenkins, "The Terminal Woodland–Mississippian Transition in West and Central Alabama," *Journal of Alabama Archaeology* 49, nos. 1–2 (2003): 1–62.

8. John H. Blitz, *Ancient Chiefdoms of the Tombigbee* (Tuscaloosa: University of Alabama Press, 1993).

9. Jenkins, "The Terminal Woodland–Mississippian Transition in West and Central Alabama"; C. Margaret Scarry, "Domestic Life on the Northwest Riverbank at Moundville," in *Archaeology of the Moundville Chiefdom,* ed. Vernon James Knight, Jr., and Vincas P. Steponaitis (Washington, DC: Smithsonian University Press, 1998), 63–101.

10. Jenkins, "The Terminal Woodland–Mississippian Transition in West and Central Alabama."

Chapter 4

1. Mary Lucas Powell, "Of Time and the River: Perspectives on Health during the Moundville Chiefdom," in *Archaeology of the Moundville Chiefdom,* ed. Vernon James Knight, Jr., and Vincas P. Steponaitis (Washington, DC: Smithsonian Institution Press, 1998), 102–19; Margaret J. Schoeninger and Mark R. Schurr, "Human Subsistence at Moundville: The Staple-Isotope Data," in *Archaeology of the Moundville Chiefdom,* ed. Vernon James Knight, Jr., and Vincas P. Steponaitis (Washington, DC: Smithsonian Institution Press, 1998), 120–32.

2. Scarry, "Domestic Life on the Northwest Riverbank at Moundville."

3. Most of this research, conducted by Vernon James Knight, Jr., and University of Alabama students, is not yet published; see Robyn L. Astin, "Mound M: Chronol-

ogy and Function at Moundville" (M.A. thesis, University of Alabama, 1996); and Elizabeth Anne Ryba, "Summit Architecture on Mound E at Moundville" (M.A. thesis, University of Alabama, 1997).

4. This conclusion is based on Moore's description of these deposits, systematic shovel test pits at M1 in 2006, and a recent analysis of Mound W; see Pamela Anne Johnson, "The Occupational History of Mound 'W' at Moundville, Alabama" (M.A. thesis, University of Alabama, 2005).

5. Vernon James Knight, Jr., "The Institutional Organization of Mississippian Ritual," *American Antiquity* 51 (1986): 675–87.

6. Christopher S. Peebles, "Moundville and Surrounding Sites: Some Structural Considerations of Mortuary Practices," in *Approaches to the Study of Mortuary Practices,* ed. James A. Brown, Memoir 15 (Society for American Archaeology, 1971), 69–71.

7. Vernon James Knight, Jr., "Moundville as a Diagrammatic Ceremonial Center," in *Archaeology of the Moundville Chiefdom,* ed. Vernon James Knight, Jr., and Vincas P. Steponaitis (Washington, DC: Smithsonian Institution Press, 1998), 44–62.

8. See Hudson, *The Southeastern Indians.*

9. Specifically, Knight identifies the ranked kin group affiliated with a mound as a "subclan" or the local members of a clan in a particular community.

10. Vernon James Knight, Jr., "Characterizing Elite Midden Deposits at Moundville," *American Antiquity* 69, no. 2 (2004): 304–21.

11. Mound G had a higher frequency of bottles than did Mound Q.

12. Vernon James Knight, Jr., "A Preliminary Account of an Earthlodge at Moundville" (paper presented at the

60th annual meeting of the Southeastern Archaeological Conference, 2003).

13. Gregory D. Wilson, "Between Plaza and Palisade: Household and Community Organization at Early Moundville" (Ph.D. diss., University of North Carolina, 2005).

14. Ibid.

15. Scarry, "Domestic Life on the Northwest Riverbank at Moundville"; Joseph O. Vogel and Jean Allan, "Mississippian Fortifications at Moundville," *Archaeology* 38, no. 5 (1985): 62–63.

Chapter 5

1. Vernon James Knight, Jr., and Vincas P. Steponaitis, "A New History of Moundville," in *Archaeology of the Moundville Chiefdom,* ed. Vernon James Knight, Jr., and Vincas P. Steponaitis (Washington, DC: Smithsonian University Press, 1998), 1–25.

2. John H. Blitz, "The Termination of Mound X at Moundville" (paper presented at the 72nd Annual Meeting of the Society for American Archaeology, 2007); Vincas P. Steponaitis, "Excavations at 1TU50, an Early Mississippian Center Near Moundville," *Southeastern Archaeology* 11 (1992): 1–13.

3. Excavations have not penetrated to the base of the largest mounds at Moundville; it is possible that some of these mounds were in use prior to A.D. 1200, contemporary with Mound X and 1TU50.

4. Vogel and Allan, "Mississippian Fortifications at Moundville"; Blitz, "The Termination of Mound X at Moundville."

5. Scarry, "Domestic Life on the Northwest Riverbank at Moundville."

6. Knight and Steponaitis, "A New History of

Moundville." Population estimates for Moundville have ranged as high as three thousand at the site's peak of occupation.

7. Phase dates based on excavated pottery are available for many outlying mound sites, but for some of these mounds the dating remains inadequate or unknown. See Paul D. Welch, "Outlying Sites within the Moundville Chiefdom," in *Archaeology of the Moundville Chiefdom,* ed. Vernon James Knight, Jr., and Vincas P. Steponaitis (Washington, DC: Smithsonian University Press, 1998), 133–66.

8. Vincas P. Steponaitis, "Population Trends at Moundville," in *Archaeology of the Moundville Chiefdom,* ed. Vernon James Knight, Jr., and Vincas P. Steponaitis (Washington, DC: Smithsonian University Press, 1998), 26–43.

9. Wilson, "Between Plaza and Palisade."

10. Steponaitis, "Population Trends at Moundville."

11. Welch, "Outlying Sites within the Moundville Chiefdom."

12. Knight and Steponaitis, "A New History of Moundville."

13. The population loss at Moundville is not unusual. It was common for Mississippians to abandon old centers and establish new ones nearby. See John H. Blitz, "Mississippian Chiefdoms and the Fission-Fusion Process," *American Antiquity* 64, no. 4 (1999): 577–92.

14. Vincas P. Steponaitis, "Contrasting Patterns of Mississippian Development," in *Chiefdoms: Power, Economy, and Ideology,* ed. Timothy Earle (New York: Cambridge University Press, 1991), 193–228.

15. Knight and Steponaitis, "A New History of Moundville."

16. The link between political changes and changes in public buildings is presented in David G. Anderson, *The Savannah River Chiefdoms* (Tuscaloosa: University of Alabama Press, 1994).

17. Welch, "Outlying Sites within the Moundville Chiefdom."

18. Evidence that droughts had an impact on Mississippian centers is presented in David G. Anderson, David W. Stahle, and Malcolm K. Cleaveland, "Paleoclimate and the Potential Food Reserves of Mississippian Societies: A Case Study from the Savannah River Valley," *American Antiquity* 60, no. 2 (1995): 258–86.

19. Knight and Steponaitis, "A New History of Moundville."

Chapter 6

1. Information concerning this excavation block and burial is based on Peebles, "Excavations at Moundville," which is a summary of the original notes and forms on file at Moundville Archaeological Park.

2. Mississippian funeral customs were varied and complex. At Moundville, bodies were buried, dug back up, or otherwise disturbed by later activities. Many of the skeletons found in the graves are incomplete, and bits of human bone are scattered throughout middens. Bones from bodies were retained, handled, displayed in various ways, and later reburied. In societies concerned with ancestors and with no written records, human bones are a kind of "document" about the relationship between living and dead people. For Moundville, see Powell, *Status and Health in Prehistory.*

3. Peebles, "Excavations at Moundville."

4. Ibid.

5. Ibid.

6. Steponaitis, "Population Trends at Moundville."

7. Wilson, "Between Plaza and Palisade."

8. It will be obvious to some readers that much of the past, especially aspects of past societies that do not preserve, is not directly accessible to us today. While historical sciences can make many claims about the past with a high degree of confidence, all scientists acknowledge that these conclusions are probability measurements, not absolute truths. Often the probability that the claim is correct is so high (supported by evidence many times over) that scientific knowledge about the past can be accepted as "true" in any practical sense of the word. Historical fiction, even attempts to reconstruct the past as accurately as possible, has limitations as well. As creative efforts, such stories humanize a distant past and remind us of our collective heritage as human beings. However, authenticity demands that the source material comes from the historical sciences. A less obvious limitation is the fact that the culture (values, customs, and beliefs) of the societies we live in today shapes our understanding of the world. Despite our best efforts, we will project our modern cultural values back into a past that may not have had these values. None of these limitations prevents us from learning about the past.

9. Shell particles were used as temper, a binding agent that prevented the pottery from cracking. Wooden mortars and pestles continued to be used by Southeastern Indians until recent times; skeletal evidence confirms their use by Mississippians. See Patricia S. Bridges, "Skeletal Evidence of Changes in Subsistence Activities between the Archaic and Mississippian Time Periods in Northwestern Alabama," in *What Mean These Bones?*

Studies in Southeastern Bioarchaeology, ed. Mary Lucas Powell, Patricia S. Bridges, and Ann Marie Wagner Mires (Tuscaloosa: University of Alabama Press, 1991), 89–101.

10. Here we are guessing that the Moundville people, like their historic descendants, lived in groups of houses where the women were members of the same related kin group, traced through the female line (matrilineage/clan). People inherited membership in their mother's clan and could not marry others of the same clan. So the house belongs to White-Wind Mother, not Bear Paw, who is a member of a different clan.

11. As in most pre-industrial societies, there was a division of labor by gender. Left-Hand Killer has achieved adult male status by becoming a warrior and demonstrating that he can provide food to a household. He is now eligible for marriage.

12. Marriage in pre-industrial societies was about more than romantic love between individuals; alliance and economic relations between families were important. White-Wind Mother's brother Red-Wind "Uncle," the senior male of her matrilineage/clan, has more control over the marriage than does Bear Paw.

13. The striped pole is an important Mississippian symbol. There is abundant evidence that marker poles, some very large, were erected at Mississippian sites. A large posthole was found just a few feet from S-8. For Mississippian symbolism, see essays in *Hero, Hawk, and Open Hand: American Indian Art of the Ancient Midwest and South,* ed. Richard F. Townsend (Chicago: The Art Institute of Chicago, 2004).

14. Many years later, Hummingbird-girl is the senior woman in her matrilineage/clan and thus has the title of White-Wind Grandmother.

15. For this interpretation of the hand-and-eye sym-
bolism, see George E. Langford, "World on a String:
Some Cosmological Components of the Southeastern
Ceremonial Complex," in *Hero, Hawk, and Open Hand:
American Indian Art of the Ancient Midwest and South,* ed.
Richard F. Townsend (Chicago: The Art Institute of
Chicago, 2004), 207–17.